Praise for

The C.A.S.T.L.E. Method

"*The C.A.S.T.L.E. Method* is positive and supportive and addresses every aspect of having not a perfect but an excellent family."

—Dr. Phil McGraw

"*The C.A.S.T.L.E. Method* is a direct, practical, actionable guide for parents on how to build a safe, understanding, and compassionate but firm environment for children. One that accepts each child for who they are and helps parents navigate the extraordinary stress of today's reality. An absolute must-read. I wish I had had this book to guide me as a young parent."

—William Haseltine, PhD, former professor at Harvard Medical School and Harvard School of Public Health, businessman, author, and philanthropist

"Donna Tetreault's strengths—as a mom, as a journalist, and as a parenting expert—all shine in this outstanding guide to parenting that is destined to be a classic. *The C.A.S.T.L.E. Method* is packed with relatable humor, concise research, and actionable tips that will be an asset in any parent's tool belt, be they on their sixth child or just starting out."

—Michele Borba, EdD, educational psychologist, TODAY show contributor, author of *Thrivers: The Surprising Reasons Why Some Kids Struggle and Others Shine*

"Raising children today is tougher than ever. With research, wisdom, and the heart of a mother, *The C.A.S.T.L.E. Method* focuses on what matters most: love, compassion, and acceptance. Tetreault's meaningful book overflows with practical tools to help positively impact the trajectory of your parenting."

—Robin Berman, MD, author of *Permission to Parent: How to Raise Your Child with Love and Limits*

"This is a game-changing approach to parenting that leads with love, compassion, and empathy. What I love most about *The C.A.S.T.L.E. Method* is, despite its regal title, it is not written from on-high but from the practical, hands-on, been-there, 'I get it' voice of Donna Tetreault. Her lived experiences in the trenches of parenthood add such honesty, humor, and heart to this brilliant must-have parenting resource. In its pages we not only learn to teach our children about kindness but learn to be kinder to ourselves in the perfectly imperfect journey of parenthood."

—Brad Bessey, former executive producer of *Entertainment Tonight* and *The Talk*

"In our Pinterest-perfect parenting world, it can seem impossible to meet the expectations put on us as parents. Tetreault breaks down these overzealous expectations and helps us to focus on what is truly important by giving us the groundwork to build a strong foundation with our kids that isn't overwhelming or impossible."

—Eve Rodsky, author of the *New York Times* best-selling book *Fair Play*

"With wisdom and warmth, Donna Tetreault has written the parenting guidebook we've all been looking for. *The C.A.S.T.L.E. Method* draws on the author's wealth of knowledge and experience to provide welcome structure to the daunting task of raising a happy, cohesive family amidst today's unique challenges. Follow her sound strategies, and you'll have constructed an impenetrable castle."

—Jenn Curtis, MSW, educational consultant and bestselling co-author of *The Parent Compass: Navigating Your Teen's Wellness and Academic Journey in Today's Competitive World*

"I am beyond thrilled about *The C.A.S.T.L.E. Method*. This is a timely book so needed and it is unique because it covers every challenge you may encounter as a parent today. Not only does Donna illustrate through her own personal stories, but she also offers groundbreaking solutions. *The C.A.S.T.L.E. Method* shows how important it is for parents and young people to understand their unique attributes and life purpose as individuals. In a world taken by a pandemic, technology, and disconnect—*The C.A.S.T.L.E. Method* is an all-encompassing story mixed with real life parenting challenges and solutions. Donna is not only a parent but has years of expertise interviewing professionals and hearing daily about the most trending parenting concerns. This book will give you solutions and details on how to parent with a heart. Donna demonstrates beautifully the needs of our youth today. Teaching our children compassion, empathy, understanding, kindness, and most importantly, how to express their emotions is key in today's world. *The C.A.S.T.L.E. Method* is a breath of fresh air. If you are seeking solutions on how to best communicate, parent, and bond with your child, this book is for you."

—Dr. Regine Muradian, author,
family psychologist, parenting expert

"Donna Tetreault's *The C.A.S.T.L.E. Method*, will help parents feel seen and supported. Her collaborative approach—combining personal parenting anecdotes with complementary content from psychologists, parenting experts, and thought leaders that she has personally interviewed or researched—make her book timely, accessible, and full of helpful strategies that parents can apply immediately. *The C.A.S.T.L.E. Method* is geared toward parents of elementary- and middle school–aged children. I wish I had access to these insights when my own kids were younger!"

—Cynthia C. Muchnick, MA, professional speaker, educational
consultant, and author of *The Everything Guide to Study Skills, The
Parent Compass: Navigating Your Teen's Wellness and Academic Journey
in Today's Competitive World,* and *Writing Successful College Applications,* among others. www.cynthiamuchnick.com

"If you're a new parent (or even a seasoned one), and you're looking for the essential tools you need to help you raise happy, well-adjusted kids who understand compassion, acceptance, security, trust, love, and the value of expectations, *The C.A.S.T.L.E. Method* is the book for you. That's because Donna injects a lifetime of experience as an educator, a mom, and a nationally recognized parenting expert into every page."

—Lisa Sugarman, mom, nationally syndicated columnist,
radio show host, and author of *How to Raise Perfectly Imperfect Kids
and Be OK with It, Untying Parent Anxiety,* and *LIFE: It Is What It Is*

"As a mom of three, I know first-hand just how difficult being a parent can be. *The C.A.S.T.L.E. Method* is a must-read! It helps navigate the sometimes-uncertain waters of parenting with easy-to-understand and practical advice. Donna nails it with this book!"

—Susan Koeppen, Emmy award-winning journalist,
president of Susan Koeppen Media,
and the 4:00 p.m. news anchor at WPXI-TV, Pittsburgh

"These days, it's easy for kids and teens to get off track, but Donna's gentle yet effective parenting approach via *The C.A.S.T.L.E. Method* is perfect for navigating parenting pitfalls in today's social media– and tech-driven world. As a journalist, educator, and mom, Donna injects real-world experience and research into her book, which produces tangible results in her own family and will also help you raise happy, healthy, well-adjusted kids."

—Stephanie Stanton, national TV host/correspondent
and parent of two young children

"*The C.A.S.T.L.E. Method* comes at a time when the need for caring leaders is more important than ever. Packed with an abundance of tools, strategies, and solutions, this book provides parents with a powerful framework in which to raise the next generation of children to become the caring, empathetic, and compassionate leaders that we so desperately need."

—Kristi Rible, founder and CEO of The Huuman Group
and Stanford instructor of Motherhood & Work

THE
C.A.S.T.L.E.
METHOD

Published by Familius LLC, www.familius.com
PO Box 1249, Reedley, CA 93654

Familius books are available at special discounts for bulk
purchases, whether for sales promotions or for family or
corporate use. For more information, contact Familius Sales
at orders@familius.com.

Some names have been changed to protect privacy.

Library of Congress Control Number: 2021952011

Print ISBN 9781641706643
Ebook ISBN 9781641706698
Printed in the United States of America

Edited by Tina Hawley and Spencer Skeen
Cover design by Derek George
Book design by Maggie Wickes

10 9 8 7 6 5 4 3 2 1

First Edition

FOREWORD BY DR. PHIL McGRAW

THE
C.A.S.T.L.E.
METHOD

Building a Family Foundation on
Compassion, Acceptance, Security, Trust,
Love, and Expectations + Education

DONNA TETREAULT

To my wonderfully supportive and patient husband, Andrew. Thank you for always believing in me.

To my beautiful babies, Jackson and Asher. You are my inspiration. You are my everything.

I love you all with every piece of my heart.

Contents

Foreword

by Dr. Phil McGraw

Donna Tetreault is my dear friend and respected colleague. Having worked shoulder to shoulder with Donna for many years, I have had the privilege of watching *The C.A.S.T.L.E. Method: Building a Family Foundation on Compassion, Acceptance, Security, Trust, Love and Expectations plus Education* evolve into what it is today. I have seen family after family claim victory by embracing Donna's philosophies and specific action plans. I've seen it in her television work, read it in her blogs, columns, and book, *Dear Me: Letters to Myself for All of My Emotions*, and recognize it in her lesson plans as a teacher. Building strong families is in her DNA. Donna Tetreault is the real deal. She is compassionate and committed and is absolutely the best parenting expert and family advocate I have ever encountered. And she has a great sense of humor too!

I believe *The C.A.S.T.L.E. Method* can be the critically important vehicle for your parenting path. Why? I believe children need nurturance right now but also a steady hand to help relaunch them into active, competitive social and academic life. Donna is on top of parenting trends and addresses everything parents want and need to know—right now.

We can no longer wait to fix mental health issues as they arise; we must be proactive in providing positive mental health strategies early on in our children's lives. The research indicates this clearly: the CDC statistics reveal that young people today are experiencing higher levels of depression, anxiety, and loneliness than at any time prior to now. To that end, teaching our children early on about their mental health, self-love, and self-compassion is a theme that runs throughout this entire book and that must be present in parenting and family life.

We not only want successful children and families, we want healthy children and families. The toll the pandemic has taken on families across America, parents and children alike, is profound. The impact is mental, emotional, educational, personal, social, and developmental. *The C.A.S.T.L.E. Method* is positive and supportive and addresses every aspect of having not a perfect but an excellent family. There could not be a more relevant time for the release of Donna's book than *right now!*

The C.A.S.T.L.E. Method's power reflects Donna's layered combination of years of experience, training, compassion, and a commitment to evidence-based approaches to parenting in every context. Donna has dedicated her career to figuring out best practices in parenting, knowing and understanding that no one child or parent is the same. As a result, she has been able to identify what matters most in the development of a child and in practicing parenting to ensure the best care for our children. Simply put, Donna gets it. She is a mom in the trenches right now with two tween boys. She is no theoretician; she is a real-world hands-on parent, and she understands and empathizes with the challenges in today's parenting.

This book is the answer to prayer for every parent who ever threw up their hands in exasperation, saying, "I love these children, but oh how I wish they had come with a manual, a set of instructions, some how-tos!" I urge you, dear reader, to take what Donna has learned and give gentle advice and instruction to your own children, fulfilling Donna's wish—and no doubt your own—that children will truly be the beneficiaries of her work.

Introduction

On January 16, 2008, at 7:12 a.m., Dr. Paul Hackmeyer exclaimed, "It's a boy!" and my life changed forever. I was no longer just Donna; I was now a mother to Jackson. By my side that day was my own mother, the most loving and caring mom a child could ever ask for. She was the person who loved me most in the world, unconditionally, and I felt that love every day of my life.

I have so many great memories of how my mother parented me. I keep them in mind always. She was so friendly, loving, and fun. I was not like her. I was extremely shy. But she saw me. She really saw me.

When I was just a little girl in preschool, she gently helped me make friends. I can recall her suggesting that we go to our neighbor's house to visit. She stayed nearby while I played with the little girl next door. She always pushed me in order to help me, but in a way that wasn't so scary. She instinctively knew I was a very different person than she was, and she honored that. She taught me to want the best for my own children, just as she had wanted for me. She taught me to enjoy the process.

My mother had been suffering from early onset Parkinson's disease for over fifteen years. We didn't know it then on that sunny, wintery day when my baby first arrived, but I would only have my mom with me on this earth for another five years.

My second son, Asher, came just a year after Jackson. I was busy taking care of my two babies during that time, and now my mom really needed me too. Slowly losing my mother and being a new mom at the same time was one of the most difficult experiences of my life. I felt sad and alone even though she was still with us. She couldn't do what we had always dreamed about doing together: picking up kids from school together, having Sunday dinners with the whole family, and just enjoying life together. All I could do was hold sacred our connection, our time as mother and daughter, even as I knew our time would likely be limited. She was the one person I needed to teach me how to be a mom, and she was slipping away from me. So in the time we had left, I listened diligently to her counsel, and I watched her closely as she engaged with her other grandchildren. When her illness grew more serious, I had to think back to my childhood for all the lessons she had taught me rather than getting her advice in the present. I still think about those days often.

I frequently recall her sweet smile and see that same smile in my Asher. I tell him he has Nonna's smile. I know she is guiding me in spirit. I hear her loud and clear, and I still write to her to this day. Here's a note I wrote to her on her birthday, November 3, in 2019, when I was in the process of writing this book:

> *Dear Mom, my beautiful, sweet angel,*
>
> *Everything you taught me, everything you showed me, all that you imagined for me is inspired in the words that come next on these pages. I am forever grateful for your lessons and love. Thank you for allowing me to be me. You are always with me.*
>
> *I love you with all my heart,*
>
> *Donna*

Those first years were just the start of my personal parenthood journey. They were hard and sometimes confusing—but incredibly rewarding—and I know I'm not alone in my experience. The reality is that we know nothing about parenting until we are in it and living it, year to year, month to month, day to day, hour to hour, and even minute to minute. Just when you think you've got it, you realize you don't—or maybe you do . . . just a little. A strong, uninterrupted learning curve can feel nearly unattainable. Parents everywhere do their best to make sure their children are on the right track, but sometimes life can get overwhelming and muddy (literally) and the best of intentions can go awry. Sometimes all that dirt ends up in a war of words in a Facebook post. Welcome to today's parenting!

The fact is that we learn how to parent as we go, drawing on a variety of sources, from parents who walked the walk before us to professional scientists researching child development. The trick is how to educate ourselves, how to choose what sources to rely on, and how much to rely on them, especially when they contradict each other. I'm sure you've heard the noise:

"Step back. Don't be a helicopter parent."

"Push."

"Don't push."

"Don't yell. Whisper."

Really, whisper? I tried that . . . it doesn't work. Yelling doesn't work either. There are so many experts in the field trying to put together the best way to raise a child, but there is no *one way*, no *perfect solution*. Every parent on the planet—be they stay at home or working, single or divorced, gay or straight, celebrity or not—will struggle along the way, and for every parent on the planet, the solution to a happy, strong family will be unique. The question for parents then (and it's the question that this book attempts to answer) is this: Are there any common denominators, any general principles that will apply to all families, even if the exact application looks different for everyone?

The short answer is yes. You'll get the long answer by reading this book.

My Parenting Education

I have been digging into this subject for more than a decade. I have been talking to parents and interviewing the nation's top experts, doctors, and educators since my first son was born thirteen years ago. I am an educator turned general assignment TV reporter turned parenting TV reporter and writer. Add to the list a guest blogger for Harvard University's Graduate School of Education and parenting expert on the *Dr. Phil* show, which still feels surreal. (If my mom had been there when I got the call to appear on the show, she would have been jumping for joy. She adored Dr. Phil, and I agree. Dr. Phil's support and kindness are unmatched as are his decades of child advocacy, promoting healthy families, and tackling mental health. I'm particularly grateful that he has agreed to write the foreword to this book.)

Before I started reporting, I was a teacher. After earning a BA in English from UCLA, I dove headfirst into teaching while earning a multiple-subject teaching credential, and for five years I taught elementary school in East Los Angeles, in the LA Unified School District. My students came from one of the lowest-income neighborhoods in the district. Each of their parents worked, maybe two or three jobs. There were lots of kids in the classroom but not a whole lot of resources. Being a teacher gives you quite a perspective on children and parenting.

Parents wanted to help their children do better in school and better in life, but they didn't always know how. One parent asked me to make sure her son got his homework done. That was not my job, but she didn't know how to get him motivated at home. She didn't understand how vital her role in her son's education was, how important it was that we were a team—Student, Teacher, and Parent. I've since come to find out that she is not alone. Many parents lack the time and resources to sufficiently involve themselves in their children's education, and this is just one of the problems parents face.

I did enjoy teaching. I loved the kids. Still, there weren't a lot of resources, and I wasn't sure teaching was the right fit for me. So I decided to make a career change from teaching to reporting. That change turned my world upside down and east toward Midland, Texas, market 145. After that, I moved to Rochester, New York, market 76. And after only four short years, which at the time felt like forever, I finally made my way back to Los Angeles. I made it home.

Reporting in LA is not for the faint of heart. It is a grueling existence. The very first news director to hire me in LA introduced me to the KCBS-TV managing editor (the person who hands out the assignments) and said seven words I'll never forget: "Sink or swim, give her a story." With that, my LA reporting career began.

I quickly became KCBS-TV's education reporter. After a few years, I moved on to KNBC-TV (trading a weekend work schedule for a weekday one). I spent eight years there and was living the dream. After I got my national break, I started working weekends again at CNN in the Los Angeles bureau.

I loved TV reporting, but not for the reasons you might think. It's hard work, and there's no glory in it. That two to three minutes you see on air takes hours and hours of work. Fortunately, what I enjoyed most was interviewing people, getting their stories, and highlighting what mattered most. I also really enjoyed putting words to pictures, crafting a story, and giving viewers important and accurate information. Journalists are tasked with finding the truth and educating the public. That's what made me tick. The digging, the hunger for knowledge—that's what made it the best job in the world . . . until I became a mom.

Breaking news from 2007: we were finally pregnant! And with that, I knew my reporting career was no match for my imminent new role. I had always wanted to be a mom. We had tried for years to become pregnant, even while a blood clotting disorder led to four miscarriages and a lot of sadness and grief. But doctors eventually figured it out, and I was finally able to bring a baby to term. You already know a bit of what happened next, so let's fast forward a little to 2008.

Jackson was six months old at the time, and I was pregnant with my second baby, Asher. I was like every other new mom: exhausted, worried, and just trying to keep it together. Once Asher arrived, I was in it deep. I knew I needed to learn more about parenting. I wanted to know what parents in the home and experts in the field knew. I wanted to hear the good, the bad, and the ugly. I was a sponge, just like my little babies. That's when I decided I'd focus on parenting reporting. I'd take my skill set and use it to educate myself and anyone else who wanted to know more about kids, families, and parenting.

And boy oh boy, did I get schooled! As a TV reporter, I had access to an amazing amount of information. I could talk to educators at Stanford, Harvard, and UCLA; psychologists; researchers; doctors in the nation's best hospitals; celebrities; coaches; teachers in preschool, elementary school, and high school; regular moms and dads; grandparents—the list goes on and on, and I asked them question after question. I asked researchers what they have proven to work. I asked parents about when they have failed and how they might have done it differently. Of course I asked them about their children; that's the best part, when parents light up about their kid and share the joy! For me, that's what life is all about. I have been so blessed to have these people and their knowledge in my life, and you will get little bits of wisdom from all those interviews as you read this book.

This unique experience as a teacher, general assignment reporter, parenting reporter, and mom gives me a complex, interesting perspective. I have practiced parenting, just as many parents have and do. I probe, I test, and when I find good results, I put a plan into action. I practice, practice, practice, day in and day out. But I have also studied parenting and family in depth for the past twelve years, and I continue to study. I want this book to showcase what I have learned as a mom to my two sons, Jackson and Asher, and to connect with you, parent to parent. I have interviewed literally hundreds of people and asked thousands of questions. I asked the questions all parents have, and because of my job, I could get the most accurate, timely, and effective answers. These are the kinds of answers that allow for actionable solutions, that can change lives for the better: mine, yours, and our children's. My digging has shifted who my husband and I are as parents. I am a real mom to two boys in the trenches, right now. I bring what I learn into my home and make it work for us, and I want to share my experiences: the successes, the failures, but most of all the love.

As you read, remember that you don't ever have to feel guilty about your parenting efforts. "Mommy guilt," or parent guilt, is a term that should never be uttered again as far as I'm concerned. You are doing your best. You are where you are in your journey. So please be gentle with yourself. Keep in mind, my dear sweet parents, that you too are learning and growing as this journey unfolds. Perhaps you are building a family for the first time, and you've never done anything like this ever before. Perhaps you're a few years or even a few decades down the road, and you're looking for a way to start over. To you, I say, "Better late than never!" This book is also for grandparents, stepparents, legal guardians, and anyone else looking to develop their parenting skills.

No matter your background or family configuration, this book is for you too. For simplicity, I alternate between the traditional pronouns "he/him" and "she/her" when referring to children and teens in the singular. Parents are referred to in the plural: "they" or "you." However, I hope people of all genders will read and benefit from what I have to offer. Regardless of where you are on your parenting journey, your needs and wants matter. Everyone in your family has the right to grow into the best version of themselves, as parents and children, both as individuals and as a family. That includes you.

I, for one, am always learning and growing, trying to be the best parent I *can* be. I've learned to focus on creating the best family I can create, rather than on what I think the perfect family *should* be. And as I've applied the principles I've learned as a parent, a teacher, and a reporter, I've seen the benefits in my own family. But please remember this: what works for one family does not always work for another family. No one parent or child is the same. Repeat: no one parent or child is the same. One more time: no one parent or child is the same. The point of this book is to provide general principles that can be applied to any family, so think as you read about how your specific circumstances will affect your decisions.

Here's another important note: I believe in teaching children very early in life, since it gives them a solid foundation. That foundation, in fact, is the basis of this book. Much of the advice I give here is tailored to families with younger children. I believe deeply in my soul that the earlier you begin, the better the results. But this foundational work can be used in older families too. If you are reading now as a parent to tweens or teens, the same principles apply. You can change how you parent at any time. You can change your perspective. You can start anytime you want to create the best version of your family.

You know your kid better than anyone else. No one else can even come close. Ever. I believe if parents are doing their best, that best is good enough. A child can feel that effort and all the love behind it. I want parents to feel confident, just as they do in other aspects of their lives. It's possible, and it's peaceful. I'm not here to take your place. I'm just here to pass on what I've learned and what has worked for me so that you can take what works for you and use it to strengthen your family. That peaceful result is why I created the CASTLE Method.

The CASTLE Method Explained

The CASTLE Method will give you the tools to be confident in your parenting choices, to know that you are focused on the right goals, even if life doesn't always go perfectly. My definition of a castle is a sanctuary, a tower of strength, a protection, a great house, a beautiful retreat safe against intrusion or invasion. I use this acronym, CASTLE, as a metaphor for building a magnificent life with your children and founding a family that thrives. This method is not about achieving your fantasy of a perfect life; it's about building the castle and experience that works for you and your children. There are so many wonderfully spectacular castles in the world, and none of them is the same.

Now I want you to envision your castle, the safe, compassionate, and loving castle you want to provide for your children. This castle will allow your children to expand into everything they are meant to do and be, knowing that they are always evolving and that it's your job, as parents, to guide and support them as they create their own path in the world.

My castle is far from perfect—*no one is perfect in our castle*—but it is a happy place, most of the time. I even designed a literal secret garden in

art by Jackson Bunnin

my backyard where we can remind ourselves to start with compassion and find calm in times of struggle, because those times always come, to everyone. This book is filled with my real-life struggles and successes in parenting, my difficult stories as well as my inspirational ones. I hope that any parent who reads this book begins to feel self-compassion and self-love in their role as parent. It's the best feeling in the world when you can take a step back, love yourself for all you are doing as a parent, and be at peace with all you've done.

But this book isn't just a comfort read. I created the CASTLE Method as a guide for parents, a blueprint that is as clear as it can be in the world of parenting. In short, what I have come to understand in my twelve years of study is there are certain foundational building blocks that are vital for children to develop and truly thrive. Each chapter in this book will be a deep dive into one of these building blocks, each assigned one of the letters in CASTLE:

- Compassion
- Acceptance

- Security
- Trust
- Love
- Expectations + Education

Compassion is first on the list because it is the foundation of all that comes after. Compassion is what sets up all interactions between family members. As parents, we all want to guide our children and support them in their respective lives, but sometimes we just get in our own way. It's like we can't help ourselves. But we can learn to have a mindset that allows for our children's varied development by understanding that our children are truly works in progress. Building a foundation while focusing on compassionate parenting, in my mind, is a real and impactful part of our role as parents and the formation of a child and family. Compassion is essential in all we do. But a person is not born with a fixed amount of compassion; we can nurture it and practice expressing it to those we love. Science tells us this (more on that in chapter 1!).

After compassion, I discuss acceptance, security, trust, love, expectations, and education in turn. And the information you'll encounter will be easy to follow. (As a TV reporter with years of experience, I know how to break down information and make the research simple and applicable.) Along with my personal stories, you'll get the latest research on child development, education, and innovative parenting concepts. I've interviewed the top experts in the parenting field, collecting best practices and guidance from educators, doctors, psychologists, and regular parents, all of whom provide knowledge and experience you can learn from. I've also included "Pro Parenting Tips" sections in each chapter that list quick, easy ways to apply what you're learning inside your own castle.

I want you to know you can become the Pro Parent you seek to be. This is about empowering you to the best version of yourself as a parent. I've got you! So sit back, relax, and really take in the specific foundational building blocks as I explain them. As we become more mindful of them, it becomes easier to parent, to let go and allow kids to exist as they are. Whether you're dealing with a toddler's tantrum, an unhappy experience, or just a stressful day, I hope you will think "CASTLE," and then reframe how you choose to parent.

Use the CASTLE Method each day in your home. This focus guides you to take little steps toward compassion, peace, and understanding both of yourself as a parent and of your child. Keep this book out on the kitchen counter or on your desk at home or work, so it can serve as a reminder that you have the power to create the castle, and the family, of your dreams. I've never met a parent who didn't want the absolute best for their children and family; what makes the difference is whether we decide to truly focus our efforts and make our dreams a reality. I believe every parent can be the parenting expert in their family. The CASTLE Method is what guides me, and I believe it can guide you too. Enjoy the construction and the journey. Focus on building a foundation that will withstand all the challenges life has to offer, knowing the challenges are just part of laying that foundation, the foundation which will get you to your dream castle and the family you've always imagined.

Chapter 1:

Compassion

Let us fill our hearts with our own compassion—towards
ourselves and towards all living beings.
—Thich Nhat Hanh

I was at a rival school campus for a fourth-grade basketball game. I was late (blame it on LA traffic). I rushed to find my way to the gym to try and sneak in before Jackson realized I had missed the tip-off. It's serious business if you live in my house. But as I ran through two parking lots and several buildings on my way to the gym, almost out of breath and clearly disheveled, I passed by the school's lost and found. I saw something there that struck me. It had nothing to do with basketball and everything to do with parenting, at least in my eyes.

The lost and found was a huge closet, larger than the biggest walk-in closet I've ever seen. The door was open, and there were parents rifling through the contents of what seemed to be a sea of discarded and lost jackets, sweatshirts, water bottles, and lunch boxes. It was a mess.

One exasperated parent said to her daughter in a stern tone, "You'd better find your sweater. I'm not buying another one, and it's going to be cold this winter."

Another parent shouted jokingly to me, "Do you need any water bottles?"

I must admit I giggled as I flew by because I too have visited the lost and found searching for my boys' water bottles and sweatshirts.

And then it struck me: parents everywhere are begging their children to bring home their water bottles and lunch boxes. It finally clicked that I'm not alone. I'm not the only parent feeling like my children don't listen to me, that they are ignoring me, that they don't care about the money I spend buying new water bottles. But I should have realized sooner that there are ways to avoid that frustration altogether, because I knew I had the knowledge to change how I parented in this particular instance. Why? Because I had learned so much about a child's developing brain and executive function from neurologists and educators. And that knowledge allows for a more compassionate mindset.

Compassion is a vital, foundational principle for strong, happy families, and it has many applications. Not least among them is that parents need to have compassion not only for their children, but also for themselves. I'm practicing self-compassion as I write these words. It has taken me quite a few years to write this book. In fact, there have been several iterations. But I feel confident that *The C.A.S.T.L.E. Method* is now in its best form. I don't take lightly what I am proposing to you. Please know, dear reader, I have compassion for you as well. I know how difficult and exhausting parenting can be. But I also know how beautiful and inspirational it is. As I see it, compassion is where you start as a parent, and it's where you end. But it's not always easy to be compassionate. Your ability to do so is a work in progress, and it will always be. Take courage. The true practice of compassion is life enhancing. In fact, it can be life altering.

The Value and Power of Compassion

Nelson Mandela once said, "Our human compassion binds us the one to the other—not in pity or patronizingly, but as human beings who have learnt how to turn our common suffering into hope for the future."[1] That human beings benefit from having compassion might seem like common sense, but even medical professionals often forget its importance.

"Medical school training places a strong emphasis on the attainment of knowledge—with minimal attention given to the teaching of compassion. This lack of attention to compassion in the medical field has been reported by patients, with one survey indicating that only 53% of hospitalized patients reported experiencing compassionate care."[2] Children in particular can be affected: The US Department of Health and Human Services has reported referrals for the maltreatment of 6.6 million children.[3] And the World Health Organization identifies three risk factors for child maltreatment: (1) children under the age of four, (2) children who are unwanted or who fail to meet parent expectations, and (3) children with special needs.

As a patient advocate for my mother for many years, I saw first-hand the vital role compassion plays in the medical field. We—she and our family—heard and felt hope whenever a doctor, nurse, or medical assistant showed us all compassion. But when compassion wasn't present, it was detrimental. It hurt her mentally, and it hurt her spiritually. Compassion can be defined as "a sensitivity to the suffering in self and others, with a commitment to try and alleviate or prevent it."[4] Of that definition, child psychologist James N. Kirby said, "Note that the prevention of suffering is important to compassionate motivation."[5] Understanding this active element of compassion can help parents stay on the compassionate track when dealing with difficult situations.

So how do we facilitate more compassionate family environments? How can we as parents become more enlightened? How can we understand our children better? As with many aspects of parenting, we first have to learn to have compassion for ourselves.

Getting a Compassionate Mindset

The next few sections are to help you get into the right mindset to have compassion for yourself first, as a parent, as an individual, and in any other role you play in life. Once you have that insight, you can move toward developing and showing compassion for your child. So let's start with how mindfulness and gratitude are both links toward finding and feeling self-compassion.

Mindfulness and Meditation

Every single day for the past three years, in the rush of the busy morning, my family takes a pause to check in with our mental health. We call it the "Van Alden prayer." I'll explain more about that in just a bit.

Now, Jackson and Asher often make it easy to get out of the house, into the car for carpool, and in class on time, but sometimes we don't get the easy, breezy morning we'd all love to enjoy. And so, sometimes, we have to just hit the rewind button and start off fresh. Right now, let's rewind back to partway through 2018.

It was about 7:10 a.m. on a Monday morning. We were already late by ten minutes, and the boys were arguing over socks. Yes, socks. They literally have dozens and dozens and dozens of socks, but they both needed blue socks to wear with their school's sports uniform. Jackson grabbed the socks first, and with that they were both yelling. The Monday morning mayhem just elevated to another level.

I tried to find another pair of the perfect blue socks. Jackson even tried to help. My husband, Andrew, found a few other pairs of blue socks, but Asher said they weren't right. After a while, Asher ended up with the blue socks Andrew had worn the day before.

Really? I thought. But I took a deep breath and said, "Well, if that's what you want to do, they're your feet."

But it wasn't only the socks that created chaos that morning: it was scrambling to be on time for our carpool, making sure they ate a good breakfast . . . you know exactly what I am talking about. I was exasperated, and so were the boys. They were going to start the day off in a negative way, feeling stressed and stuck.

After a few really tough mornings like this one, full of real-life pressures and hot heads, I decided we had to make a change. For ideas, I quickly thought about where I find peace . . . and that's with God.

This is when I decided I needed to really lean in to practicing mindfulness and meditation for real. First for myself and then for and with my kids. When I found my way to meditating every day, compassion was bountiful for me, my husband, and my boys. And it's not just me either. Research shows that having God in your life—or for the nonreligious, simple mindfulness and meditation—is good for you and your child.

There are many definitions of these two concepts, but for our purposes, it is easy to borrow Dr. Joshua Schultz's method of describing mindfulness as a "quality" and meditation as a "practice." So, if "meditation is a practice," as he says, then "through this practice, one can develop different qualities, including mindfulness."[6]

Mindful meditation has found its way into some innovative schools as a way to curb poor behavior, stress, and other difficult situations in the classroom. At Baltimore's Robert W. Coleman Elementary, detention has been tossed out and replaced with meditation. Teachers now send kids to what's known as the "mindful moment room." Here's how it works. A child is behaving poorly. Why? There are so many potential reasons: lack of sleep, lack of nutrition, stress in the home, lack of self-regulation—whatever the reason, a child now goes to practice mindful meditation instead of going to detention. And a child who goes to the mindful meditation room gets a moment to just breathe. She gets a second chance. Further, mindfulness isn't limited to troubled students. At the beginning and end of every school day, all kids spend fifteen minutes participating in a school-wide guided meditation session.

Since the program was put into practice, there has been a sharp decrease in referrals, and suspensions have dropped to zero. In an interview with CNN, a Robert W. Coleman student who had been ejected from his classroom after getting into a fight said that he went to the mindful moment room, "did some deep breathing, had a little snack, and I got myself together," before going back and apologizing to his class.[7] What a gift: a new way to look at oneself in the world.

Evidence indicates that it can take a child just six to seven minutes to refocus and find calm in place of perpetuating negative feelings and frustration. According to UCLA's Mindful Awareness Research Center, "research in mindfulness has identified a wide range of benefits in different areas of psychological health, such as helping to decrease anxiety, depression, rumination, and emotional reactivity. Research has also shown mindfulness helps to increase well-being, positive affect, and concentration."[8]

Children who are raised with religious or spiritual practices have ample opportunity to practice meditation, particularily in the form of prayer, both within their family and in connection with a spiritual community. In addition to the immediate benefits of prayer and meditation, research shows that kids and teens who are raised with religious or spiritual practices tend to have better physical health and mental health as they age. A Harvard study supporting this was published in the American Journal of Epidemiology in 2018.[9] Significantly, that study's findings show that it wasn't only about how much people went to religious services; it was also about how much they prayed or meditated on their own. People who prayed or meditated every day were better able to process their feelings and were more satisfied in life.[10]

So let's get back to the "Van Alden prayer" now. Each morning on our way to school, it takes my family about eight minutes to drive down Van Alden Avenue. Eight minutes driving through our neighborhood filled with beautiful oak trees, greenery, flowers that pop in the spring, and a golf course. Nature is everywhere. There are very few stop signs, and traffic flows nicely. For the most part, you don't hear much honking or see cars speeding down the hill. People walk their cute dogs, and groups of moms hike the hills together. We can turn down the radio, and there are no devices in the car, other than my phone mounted to the dashboard. The bottom line is that this part of our commute is one of the best times for us to pray, one of our family's forms of mindfulness.

So how does it work? Well, we begin with three prayers. First is one of the most common and well known: the Lord's Prayer. Next, we say the Hail Mary, and then we each share our own personal prayer. Some days we pray for what we need. You can imagine how the boys pray for help to do well in an upcoming test or in a game after school. We also share our gratitude. We talk about what we are thankful for.

Sometimes I use my prayer to show them how to pray for what they need most. As a mom, I do pray a lot for patience. I might say something like this: "God, please help me have the patience I need to be a good mother, a good wife, and a good friend. Help me stop and take a breath before I react, before I regret my words or actions." In this way, I can share my personal prayer, and they get exposure to one way to pray and be mindful. It's five times a week, consistently, all throughout the school year. And as the boys have gotten older, many nights we also practice meditation through prayer. Five to six minutes—that's it.

As a Catholic family, we also regularly attend mass, which gives us a chance to practice mindfulness through prayer and our church community. According to that Harvard study, about 18 percent of those who attended religious services at least once a week, as children or teens were more likely to report being happier in their twenties than those who had never attended services. And even more interesting to me, those who attended services were 30 percent more likely to do volunteer work and 33 percent less likely to use drugs. This last statistic is particularly significant to our parenting as a research-backed way to help our children avoid drug abuse. Religious attendees were also less likely to have sex at an earlier age or get a sexually transmitted infection.

"These findings are important for both our understanding of health and our understanding of parenting practices," said study author Ying Chen in an interview. "Many children are raised religiously, and our study shows that this can powerfully affect their health behaviors, mental health, and overall happiness and well-being."[11]

To reap these benefits, consider your own spiritual and/or religious background and decide how you would like to integrate prayer, meditation, or other mindful practices into your family.

Pro Parenting Tips: Mindful Meditations

- Pray! Consider naming your own prayer, like ours, "The Van Alden Prayer."
- Take a break in a quiet place, and just breathe, listening to your breath.
- Practice mindful awareness during the day: while cooking, while listening to music, while doing any activity. For example, I love watering in my garden. While I water the plants and flowers, I pay close attention to the water's sound, the plants getting wet, the colorful birds singing, the cool breeze at my back, and the heat of the sun.

If you want to teach your children meditation, I've included here two 10-minute meditations designed for kids.

Clouds in the Sky Meditation (from Dr. Judy Ho). Dr. Ho took me through this meditation when I interviewed her in 2020.[12] "Don't let sticky thoughts be your reality," she said then. "Just let your thoughts happen and let them move in and out of your mind like clouds moving in the sky."

- Close your eyes and get in a relaxed position.
- Inhale and exhale three or four times.
- Try to picture the sky in your mind's eye. You see lots of colors and clouds. They are drifting back and forth in no regular order.
- Continue to breathe and focus on the images of the clouds.
- What thoughts are you thinking? Are you thinking about a past mistake? Are you thinking about what you must do today? Whatever you are thinking about is okay.
- Just notice your thoughts. You don't have to analyze them or figure anything out.

- Now just put some of the thoughts on the clouds. Put your first thought that pops up on the first cloud, the second thought on the second cloud, the third thought on the third cloud, and so on.
- And just like clouds drift, your thoughts are going to drift. They drift from one side to the other. Don't try to hold onto them—it's not possible to do that—so let them drift around and move around as they should in the sky.
- When a thought leaves, you don't have to follow it. Let it drift. This helps you get unstuck.
- Every time a thought you don't like pops up, imagine just letting it drift like a cloud. This is a great reminder that you are not your thoughts. Thoughts are not about you; you are in control of your thoughts. They are just like clouds in the sky.
- Now come back down from the sky and into your breath.
- Just breathe; notice your breath.
- Inhale and exhale three to four times.
- Bring yourself back to the room and be at peace with your thoughts in a cloud.[13]

Mindful Walking Practice (from Mark Bertin).[14] I love this activity for children who like to move!

- As you begin, walk at a natural pace. With each step, pay attention to the lifting and falling of your feet. Notice movement in your legs and the rest of your body. Notice any shifting of your body from side to side.
- Now, for a few minutes, expand your attention to sounds.
- Shift your awareness to your sense of smell.
- Now move to vision.
- Keep this open awareness of everything around you.

- In the last moments, come back to awareness of the physical sensations of walking. Notice your feet again touching the ground. Notice again the movements in your body with each step.[15]

An Attitude of Gratitude

Martin Seligman, a pioneer in the field of positive psychology, has remarked, "When we take time to notice the things that go right—it means we're getting a lot of little rewards throughout the day."[16] Doesn't that sound like a fun way to go about your day? And as I focus on this mantra throughout my daily life, it really becomes clearer and clearer to me that as a parent, gratitude is a gift I can give to myself as well as to my children, bringing us all closer to a compassionate mindset.

Along those same lines is another famous quote from Abraham-Hicks: "Everything is always working out for you."[17] I printed these words out and have them on my desk. I also gave my husband his own print to put on his desk, and I hung up the quote on my boys' bedroom door. You guessed it—I really like this quote!

I include positive affirmations throughout my day as a way of increasing my gratitude. Here's an example of what that might look like:

- The Van Alden prayer is my first focus on gratitude.
- I love seeing the birds in my fountain.
- I love seeing the flowers in my garden.
- I am so grateful for the teachers my boys have.
- I am so grateful to watch them play baseball and golf.
- Wow, that email just came in. Oh yes, things are always working out for me.
- Wow, that friend just texted the sweetest note: "I'm thinking of you, and I love you." I am so grateful for my friend.
- I'm so grateful for hugs and smiles from my boys.

- I'm so grateful I get to work on this book, my life's work.
- I'm so grateful my husband put the kids to bed.

See how it works? And it just goes on and on and on. As you continue to do it, it gets easier and easier. I'm not trying to paint this "Pollyanna" picture of my life (more on the Pollyanna Principle in chapter 6), but the reality is when you focus on gratitude, you get to see how much life has to offer and how fun it can be. It's how you decide to see the world and the people around you.

According to science, positive affirmations can benefit us. But, in the words of psychologist Catherine Moore, "positive affirmations require regular practice if you want to make lasting, long-term changes to the ways that you think and feel. The good news is that the practice and popularity of positive affirmations are based on widely accepted and well-established psychological theory."[18]

What does gratitude do for the brain? Educational psychologist Kori D. Miller says, "Every time a person expresses or receives gratitude, dopamine releases in the brain. Dopamine, a neurotransmitter, is produced in two areas of the brain: the substantia nigra and the ventral tegmental. The former has to do with movement and speech, the latter with reward. When a person expresses or receives gratitude, dopamine releases, thus making a connection between the behavior and feeling good. The more a person practices gratitude, the more often dopamine releases."[19]

Now let's talk about teaching gratitude to your kids. If you can get to feeling this way by practicing gratitude, imagine what it can do for your kids. In 2017, I was writing an article for Harvard's Making Caring Common Project when I had the pleasure of interviewing Dr. Milena Batanova from the Harvard Graduate School of Education.[20] Here's what I learned.

"Gratitude is a profoundly moral emotion," Dr. Batanova told me. "Appreciating what one has naturally helps with recognizing what others don't have. We know from research that gratitude is also linked to happiness and well-being. It has a lot to do with positive thinking and recognizing positive things in your life, positive people in your life." In other words, engaging in the practice of gratitude makes us feel good and makes others feel good, benefiting all involved.

There are three simple ways to get started in the practice of gratitude. First, the holiday season is a great time to kick-start the message at home. Gratitude is a theme during the holidays. Whether we are giving thanks at Thanksgiving or choosing to help others in need during Christmas, Hanukkah, or Kwanzaa, gratitude is present. But how can we continue this expression of gratitude throughout the year? The answer: practice, practice, practice. Practice gratitude every day—that's the second way. And third, begin to extend the practice of gratitude beyond your home.

In many ways, Dr. Batanova told me, "gratitude is a way of expressing humility, to show a grounded sense of self and really appreciating others, their sacrifices, however small, the nice things that other people do for us. Expressing gratitude can also be about expressing empathy, showing that you care about someone, especially in times of need. All of these things are interrelated and take practice and reflection."

Pro Parenting Tips: Get Gratitude

- Model gratitude for your kids by thanking them when they do chores without being asked.
- Every day, in the morning or after school, ask your kids what they're grateful for. Be specific: Did someone at school do something nice or smile at them?
- During dinner, go around the table and ask everyone to state positive affirmations like these: "I am lucky to have you for my brother," "I love this meal you prepared," "I am so grateful you are doing the dishes," "I love how our dogs are quietly waiting for leftovers," etc.

- Write thank-you notes to each other and to extended family. You can even write to school bus drivers, janitors, teachers, friends, or someone else your child appreciates.
- During the holiday season, emphasize special traditions that your family enjoys.
- Keep a gratitude journal. Even one sentence or word a day can make a big difference.
- Focus on solutions rather than problems, on what you can control rather than on what you can't.
- If all else fails, remember the love you feel for your family, and be grateful for that foundation.

Practicing How to Forgive

If I'm going to be completely honest with myself and with you (which up unto this point I have and will continue to be), married life for my husband and me has not always been that bed of roses we all seem to think it will be on that magical day when we say, "I do." Nothing can prepare you for the long, winding, messy, exasperating, crazy road of marriage. *Nothing.*

But before I get deeper into that, how about I start off with our love story? We were college sweethearts, on and off. Then we grew apart and didn't speak to each other for five years before we eventually came back together as a couple. In 1999, we dated for six months, got engaged, and were married six months after that. Andrew and I have now been married for twenty years. Hooray for us! Every year, we have celebrated our wedding anniversary at Casa Del Mar in Santa Monica on or close to December 2, our wedding day. FATE, FATE, FATE.

Now, our "honeymoon" period had had a great stretch. It's different for every relationship, but for us, things were easy between us when we were in the baby phase with the boys. But as our boys grew, so did our bills, and you know, if you're married, that it's not easy to escape bumps in the road. We thought when we got married that those five years apart had enabled us to mature as people and as partners. And to an extent it had. But then we became parents, after serious struggles (including that blood clotting disorder and our miscarriages), and that changed our dynamic—it changed everything. The stressors and new expectations of parenthood were different. It wasn't just about us anymore.

Sound familiar? And along with the stressors of careers and parenting, it seemed that bickering, miscommunication, and not truly reconciling would be unavoidable. It was a struggle. For our individual well-being as well as our children's well-being, we had to figure out how to forgive more easily. I knew as their mother, I had to model how to forgive in a healthier way. As a spouse, I had to learn to be more mindful in forgiving my husband, my partner in life.

Forgiveness is a skill. And when you learn how to forgive more freely and more often, life is better. A lot better. So how do you forgive yourself, your partner, and others in the best way possible for yourself, your children, and your family? I love this quote from Martin Luther King as a guide: "Forgiveness is not an occasional act: it is a permanent attitude." So what are the steps toward forgiveness?

Maureen Healy is a sought-after speaker, educator, and expert in children's emotional health. Her most recent book, *The Emotionally Healthy Child: Helping Children Calm, Center, and Make Smarter Choices*, won the Nautilus Book Award, the Book Excellence Award, and the Foreword Indies in 2019.[21] In an article for *Psychology Today*, Healy says, "I have found that parents that teach their kids how to 'really forgive' set them up to succeed and create a foundation of strength as well as self-love."[22] As for how, she lists five simple steps for actual forgiveness:

1. Acknowledge: Acknowledge what happened.
2. Experience: Experience your feelings.
3. Communicate: Say you want to forgive.

4. Forgive: State you don't want to carry the anger anymore (or frustration, guilt, or resentment).

5. Release: Let it go. Give your anger to Great Spirit (Buddha, Jesus, Source, Nature, Universe).

Healy adds, "Each of these steps must be felt from the heart but acted upon sequentially so a child learns how to truly forgive another child (parent, sister, friend). It will free their emotional body from unresolved grief, pain, sadness and hurt."[23]

I'll add one simpler step to that list, one I got from Jackson, who was twelve at the time of writing. He told me he thinks that after Step 5 should be "Just laugh!" I like that step too.

Now to extend this practice further, and to come back to the beginning of this chapter, it is easy to forgive and forget when we are in love and all is going well in our lives. But as parents—when life and all of its difficulties creep into our hearts—we must work on what we are teaching when we model an unforgiving heart. We know from research that people learn by watching others.[24] Consider the famous 1960s Bobo doll experiments. Researchers discovered that children treated the inflatable doll the same way they saw the adults treat it. For example, children who watched an adult become aggressive with the doll became aggressive as well. Meanwhile, children who watched adults treat the doll kindly imitated the kindness.[25] What we model for our children is essential to how they will develop forgiveness as a life skill.

Now let's look at the way psychologist and mindfulness teacher Dr. Jack Kornfield illustrates how to forgive. Drawing on his experience as founder of the Massachusetts Insight Meditation Society and the California Spirit Rock Meditation center, Kornfield offers a forgiveness meditation: Sit comfortably, close your eyes, and allow your breath to be natural and easy. Let your mind and body relax. Then, in his words,

> breathing gently into the area of your heart, let yourself feel
> all the barriers you have erected and the emotions that you
> have carried because you have not forgiven—not forgiven

yourself, not forgiven others. Let yourself feel the pain of keeping your heart closed. Then, breathing softly, begin asking and extending forgiveness, reciting the following words, letting the images and feelings that come up grow deeper as you repeat them. . . . "There are many ways that I have been harmed by others, abused, or abandoned, knowingly or unknowingly, in thought, word or deed." Let yourself picture and remember these many ways. Feel the sorrow you have carried from this past and sense that you can release this burden of pain by extending forgiveness when your heart is ready. Now say to yourself: "I now remember the many ways others have hurt or harmed me, wounded me, out of fear, pain, confusion, and anger. I have carried this pain in my heart too long. To the extent that I am ready, I offer them forgiveness. To those who have caused me harm, I offer my forgiveness, I forgive you."[26]

I offer these two different approaches to practicing forgiveness to allow you some room for creating what might work for your family, what might speak specifically to you. This is where we really need to walk the walk and be the leaders and role models our children need. Finding a way to forgive that works for us is imperative to the health and well-being of our family. We must be willing participants.

Pro Parenting Tips: The Power of Forgiveness

Sometimes feelings of hurt, pain, and anger can make the idea of forgiveness feel unfair, unjust, or even plain impossible. For those moments, I've included some quotes on forgiveness from poets, philosophers, and world leaders, all of whom offer up their own thoughts on what it means to forgive and why it's so important. I hope one or more resonates with you.

- "Forgiveness does not change the past, but it does enlarge the future."—Paul Boose
- "If you can't forgive and forget, pick one."—Robert Brault
- "It is easier to forgive an enemy than to forgive a friend."—William Blake
- "Always forgive your enemies—nothing annoys them so much."—Oscar Wilde
- "We read that we ought to forgive our enemies; but we do not read that we ought to forgive our friends."—Sir Francis Bacon
- "True forgiveness is when you can say, "Thank you for that experience."—Oprah Winfrey
- "To be wronged is nothing, unless you continue to remember it."—Confucius
- "Resentment is like drinking poison and then hoping it will kill your enemies."—Nelson Mandela
- "The weak can never forgive. Forgiveness is the attribute of the strong."—Mahatma Gandhi
- "The practice of forgiveness is our most important contribution to the healing of the world."—Marianne Williamson
- "I have always found that mercy bears richer fruits than strict justice."—Abraham Lincoln
- "To err is human, to forgive, divine."—Alexander Pope

Diving Deep into Empathy

"Natural Disasters"

Asher Bunnin, Grade 4

Attacks all over the world destroying everything in sight

Wildfires, hurricanes, earthquakes, floods, and tsunamis

Rebuilding everything all over again

Taking years or decades, still never the same

Spreading all over the city

Harsh attacks coming several times

Nothing to withhold it

Ramming and crashing through every building

Wiping away all that was once yours

Tragic losses and horrible times

Some don't make it out

Stay out of trouble and save everything meaningful

Be grateful for what you have left

Be proud and think you can do anything

Good attitudes will help you accomplish anything

Protect your closest things and keep going

Be prepared for another huge outbreak

Forget the past and think about the future

A new beginning means a new potential

Strive to make your community better

This poem was written by my son Asher when he was ten years old and published in "A Celebration of Poets" in 2019. I found it to be well suited to begin this section, and I hope it touched you in some way.

2020 was no ordinary year. 2020 was a year unlike any those of us on this planet have ever experienced. 2020 was a tsunami of disruption, and that disruption happened quickly. In the middle of March, every single parent all over the world was forced to parent in a pandemic. We were all trying to wrap our heads around what was befalling us. With our kids' schools closed, we had to start working from home and teaching our kids at home. What? Yes, we were now our kids' teachers. We also had to worry about our own parents and their health. We were in lockdown. We had no idea what was next. We were literally afraid for our lives and our children's lives. All that in just the last two weeks of March. The disruption hit every single one of us, and we had no idea where we were headed.

The dozens and dozens of parents I talked to were all over the map when it came to dealing with the tsunami that had befallen us. One mom would not let her child out of her house for months. She continued to say she would not allow her child back in school until there was a vaccine. Another family I talked to allowed their kids to play team sports even when the recommendation from health officials was the exact opposite. In another household, co-parents were at opposite ends of the spectrum in dealing with the pandemic, with one parent saying it was okay for her kids to see their grandparents, and the other parent saying no way! This was a disruption unlike any other, and parents were trying to figure out how they would manage it within their families.

Then another force to be reckoned with arrived on the pandemic's heels: the brutal murder of George Floyd. Floyd's death put racism in America at the forefront of the public consciousness. Protests fueled even more uncertainty. And as a parent, I for one thought, *This is our reset. We all have a lot of work ahead of us.*

The combination of these two events highlighted the disruption in life and challenged each of us in many ways. So many questions arose: How will we, as a family, work through this? What can we do to adapt? What do we need to change? What will that look like? And the solutions did not seem easy.

In addition to giving good meditation advice, Dr. Judy Ho also has great thoughts about how children handle these kinds of disruptions. During the pandemic, I interviewed Dr. Judy Ho a second time in October 2020. We couldn't meet in person, as we were all in lockdown, but we spoke by phone. She said then that disruptions can mirror a child's development: "Sometimes children will be doing very well, and then, because of various types of disruptions or stressors in their life like school or peers, or a period of identity development, or anytime when they're feeling external forces that they can't control, things can spin out of control. There are a lot of things that we don't have control over."

Our children and our families will assuredly continue to be confronted with all types of disruptions. So what can we do as parents? According to Dr. Ho, lean into empathy. "The last thing people want to do is help others when they feel stressed and overwhelmed," she says, "but that is precisely what you have to do. . . . The minute a person is able to reorient his own life to something bigger than himself and for a cause he believes in—maybe as simple as calling a friend who needs someone to listen to them—his own despair diminishes as he sees value in his own life."

Life as it was in 2020 is an example of a persistent truth: as we live our lives each day, disruptions are always going to happen, no matter how well you've prepared or thought things through. And as parents, we must learn that all the planning in the world cannot stand up to surfing that metaphorical thirty-foot wave, not even those ones like the Pipeline in Oahu, Hawaii. And so, what do you do if you're not a pro surfer who can handle the dangers of that wave? Yeah, you can try to avoid it. But in real life, it's not that easy. Still, we're going to be able to ride the wave better if we start with empathy.

The Oxford Reference dictionary defines empathy as "the ability to imagine and understand the thoughts, perspective, and emotions of another person."[27] Interestingly, a study at Michigan University shows that young people are becoming less empathetic than ever. American college students showed a "48% decrease in empathetic concern and a 34% drop in their ability to see other people's perspectives" over the last thirty years.[28] We need to teach and model empathy not only for everyday life but for the disruptions and tsunamis as well. So, start with empathy. Feel the feelings and allow yourself the time to process all of them. All feelings are okay.

The next way to handle crises, according to Dr. Ho, is to "recognize the problem/stressor and stay in the moment. Think about the problem in front of you and solve it a day at a time. You may not be able to establish a routine right away. Tackle one piece at a time and model that behavior for your children."[29]

Dealing with the unknown is one of the most difficult things to do as a human being, let alone as a child. A third way to deal with these out-of-control situations is to start with the things you can control. Ask yourself, "What can I do? What can I control? What can I change?" Dr. Ho described to me what she calls "the Problem-Solving Method," a take on cognitive behavioral therapy that helps you address critical issues in the moment: set a timer and give yourself a few minutes to brainstorm all the things you can improve in the moment right now. What can be done first? What can be done next?

A fourth way to react to a crisis has to do with the fight-flight-freeze response. We often talk about fight and flight, but don't talk a lot about freeze. The "freeze" response is when you become so overwhelmed that you are unable to do anything. You are helpless. Dr. Judy explains how the narrative might sound like "I guess I just have to wait this out," as if people in freeze mode can't think about anything else except their own suffering. Her advice is that instead of telling yourself, "Well, I guess there is nothing I can do about it," you must change the narrative, especially in the case of disruptions that go on and on. Think of one thing that you can do today to take care of yourself or to improve your situation. Ask those questions, one at a time. Dr. Ho says, "Anxiety happens when your mind is focused on the past or the future. If your mind is focused on the now/the present moment, you are better able to manage things. Think mindfulness [and] meditation, notice your thoughts, and reset."

Just know that as you learn to ride the waves, whether it be during these extraordinary and overwhelming situations or just the average, everyday stressors, your child will learn from you and follow your lead.

Getting to Know Your Child's Brain

Before we go on to more research, let's circle back to empathy for a moment. True empathy requires understanding. It's easier to empathize with yourself because you know yourself. Your children are another matter. In order to really have empathy for them, you need to understand them, physically, mentally, and spiritually, and that takes research. In this section, I've collected research that will help you be informed about your child's brain. The more you understand about how your child thinks, the easier it will be for you to empathize when that fourth (or sixth) water bottle goes missing.

I began interviewing parenting experts all over the country when Jackson and Asher were toddlers. One of the most important interviews I did during that time, and one that really gave me insight, was with Dr. Mayumi Prins, director of the BIRC (Brain Injury Research Center) Education Program at UCLA.[30] My goal in that interview was to talk about how to protect our kids from sports concussions. But after I grilled her on every aspect of concussions that I could think of, I asked her to grant me a little more time and talk to me about the teenage brain. As parents, we always hear about the moods, the risky behavior, the defiance—heck, we lived as teenagers once, so we have our own stories. Thank goodness social media wasn't part of the world when I was a teenager. But I wanted to learn how to parent my adorable toddlers, who would eventually grow into the teens so many of us fear. I figured an introductory discussion might help me ease into their tween/teen years.

Let's talk pre-teens first. Remember that messy, unorganized lost and found closet I saw those parents digging through? What is the cause of all this chaos? What is going on in those pre-teen brains that is keeping them from remembering their homework, water bottles, and lunch boxes? The answer is executive function—or in some cases, dysfunction.

Executive function and self-regulation skills enable us to plan, focus attention, remember instructions, and juggle multiple tasks. The Harvard School on the Developing Child says the following on their website:

> In the brain, the ability to hold onto and work with information, focus thinking, filter distractions, and switch gears

is like an airport having a highly effective air traffic control system to manage the arrivals and departures of dozens of planes on multiple runways. Scientists refer to these capacities as executive function and self-regulation—a set of skills that relies on three types of brain function: working memory, mental flexibility, and self-control. Children aren't born with these skills—they are born with the potential to develop them. The full range of abilities continues to grow and mature through the teen years and into early adulthood. To ensure that children develop these capacities, it's helpful to understand how the quality of the interactions and experiences that our communities provide for them either strengthens or undermines these emerging skills.[31]

Kids, just like adults, must move through the world and react to things happening all around them. And like us, they must do it with worries, obligations, and temptations lurking inside their brains. But if we invest in practice and coaching early on, we can help kids grow executive function skills that will grant them an even stronger "air traffic control system" that will serve them throughout their lives.

That practice and coaching will come most easily if you already have an open communication channel with your child. Michelle Icard is the author of Amazon best seller *Middle School Makeover: Improving the Way You and Your Child Experience the Middle School Years*.[32] In a 2018 interview with me, she gave parents tips on how to help children grow their executive function. Icard says that talking to a child, having open and honest conversations about the brain and how it is developing, is a great way to begin the process. She says, "Offer a peek behind the curtain neurologically and biologically. Don't keep it a secret. Explain and say to a child, 'You may need a little help. I'm here to offer you that help. I want to guide you to figure this out.'"[33] Once you have that line of communication, you can put the scientific knowledge to better use.

So what is going on in the brain anyway? A lot, according to scientists. The brain of a child is basically under constant construction. And according to world expert neuroscientist Jay Giedd,

> [In the teen years, this] part of the brain that is helping organization, planning, and strategizing is not done being built yet. . . . [It's] not that the teens are stupid or incapable of [doing things]. It's sort of unfair to expect them to have adult levels of organizational skills or decision making before their brain is finished being built. . . . The exuberant growth during the pre-puberty years gives the brain enormous potential. The capacity to be skilled in many different areas is building up during those times. What the influences are of parenting or teachers, society, nutrition, bacterial and viral infections—all these factors—on this building-up phase, we're just beginning to try to understand. But the pruning-down phase is perhaps even more interesting, because our leading hypothesis for that is the "use it or lose it" principle. Those cells and connections that are used will survive and flourish. Those cells and connections that are not used will wither and die.[34]

Now, let's go back to all those lost items and homework assignments one more time. How can parents help a child whose brain is still under construction? How can a parent be more compassionate? Michelle Icard explains that parents can start off by asking a child what might help him remember his homework assignments or lunchbox: "Ask kids to come up with a strategy. Let the kid be the expert here. Ask, 'What do you think is going to work for your brain?'"[35] This allows the child to invest in his success instead of being told what to do. For some kids who are visual learners, maybe a strategically placed list will work. For a more tactile learner, maybe a timer going off on a watch will help. Don't forget, what works for one kid might not work for another. And what might work one day might not work the next. It doesn't have to be the perfect plan and execution; just keep working toward success.

It may take a kid time to develop a habit so it will work from all sorts of angles.

So now that we know how much is going on in a child's pre-teen brain, what is going on in the teenage brain? Understanding the teen brain (not like a neuroscientist, but as an educated parent) can help you maintain healthy expectations and have compassion for what your teen is experiencing. Dr. Mayumi Prins started our interview with this perspective. "When teachers teach sex education to the girls and boys and explain how their bodies are going to change," she says, "they leave something out. We don't [say,] 'Oh by the way, this is what is going to go on in your brain,' which should be a part of that curriculum so kids can know what to expect and know why they are feeling a certain way. I think it helps them get through the very difficult phase of adolescence."

This idea makes a lot of sense to me. And Dr. Prins explains this further: "The frontal part of the brain, the part right behind the forehead, the frontal cortex, the executive function, comes on board the latest, and so the decision-making processes, the order and the region of the brain we utilize to make decisions as an adult, is different from the decision-making processes and connections we make as a teenager. Teenagers tend to recruit a lot of their connections from areas of the brain that are associated with emotional development, so a lot of their decisions are emotionally driven. They're not logically driven." And that makes even more sense, right?

Another well-known fact about the teen brain is the high frequency of risk-taking behavior. Dr. Prins says, "Risk-taking behavior is the normal, evolutionary development of a child. There are a lot of changes in the connectivity of the wires of the brain, so all of those are going through a lot of changes. It's time to start breaking away from parents and become more independent, so the risk needs to be present." But teens still need direction from parents. Teens need to be aware that they might not be making the right decisions. Teens need to take risks in order to feel safe to go out into the world and be productive citizens.

Michele Icard explains it this way:

> In adolescence, kids must start taking risks, [as a way of]
> saying, "I'd like to get a job, drive a car, make some money,
> and not rely on my parents." But if the part of the brain that
> is good about thinking and being analytical stays in control
> in adolescence, it would say, "Eh, I don't really need to do
> those things. I've got it good. I don't have to pay rent, all my
> food is bought for me, and I have an Xbox [and] a comfy
> bed. Why would I take the giant risk of taking care of myself
> when I'm already being well cared for?" The emotional part
> of the brain must get dialed up so that kids can start to learn
> how to take risks, but healthy risks.[36]

That's the key: healthy risks. Teenagers need to be aware that they
might not be making the right decisions or taking the right risks.
Parents still need to be present but not in charge of all decision making.
This is the time to be the passenger, not the driver, and let your teens
travel toward adulthood.

Let's go back to the definition of compassion. It literally means
"to suffer together."[37] Emotion researchers define compassion as the
feeling that arises when you are confronted with another's suffering
and feel motivated to relieve that suffering: "Compassion is not the
same as empathy or altruism, though the concepts are related. While
empathy refers more generally to our ability to take the perspective of
and feel the emotions of another person, compassion is when those
feelings and thoughts include the desire to help."[38]

Therefore, our practice of compassion for our children plays a significant role in their everyday lives, their growth, and their development.
Truly understanding where our children are in a given moment as a
result of their developing brains is vital. Compassion is empathizing,
understanding, and working toward solutions with them. And the key
here is helping them, not "fixing" them or the situation, just plainly,
truly being there to support them.

So how can we use compassion in our daily lives to support our kids' changing brains? The starting point is always to begin with compassion, even when you feel exasperated or tired. Recognize your emotions, take a few breaths, or remove yourself from the room if you can't begin with compassion. When you are ready, start over with compassion. Trust the child/adolescent brain research. Know that everything your child is going through is normal. Trust that your child must go through the process and, with your help and guidance, will learn how to become a productive citizen. It's just part of the journey. Trust yourself and your child (more on how to do that in chapter 4!). Also make sure your child, especially if she's a teen, is getting eight to ten hours of sleep a night. This is imperative.

Parents, it's okay to be frustrated, but don't give up on your teen. We all must remember that the vast majority of people become great functioning adults, pay their bills, go to jobs, and generally thrive in life. Your kid will get there, so sit back, take a breath, and ask yourself, "What can I do in this process to get my teen to the next level?"

And while we focus on compassion, we can also help develop the increasing complexity of their executive function skills. Help kids find what feels right to them in tasks and schoolwork, at a level that will stretch them, not frustrate them. Remember that your teen's brain is under *serious* construction. Find ways for him to help himself, to help in the best development of his own brain. Focus on ownership. Dr. Jay Giedd says, "So, if a teen is doing music or sports or academics, those are the cells and connections that will be hard-wired. If they're lying on the couch or playing video games . . . those are the cells and connections that are going to survive."[39] The teenage years are challenging; there's no getting around it. But understanding what your child is going through can ease the pain.

Remember to talk to your child about her developing brain. Give your child, pre-teen, or teen the information that she needs to feel aware and educated. You can say, "Your brain will continue to grow and change through early adulthood. This is what's going to happen as you grow and develop, and it's normal and it's okay." Explain that she is not alone, that this is not only happening to her. Allow for mistakes and growth. And repeat, repeat, repeat. This is an ongoing conversation.

Pro Parenting Tips: Children with Executive Functioning Difficulties

Executive functioning difficulties in children can impact academic achievement, among many other effects. These recommendations (from professional psychologists!) are for parents with children who may experience such difficulties. Check out their website in the footnote for even more tips or see the section on "Homework Hassles" in chapter 7 of this book.[40]

- Provide structure by teaching rules and providing expectations surrounding their homework.
- Prompt your child to review his or her homework once it is completed.
- Work alongside your child when needed.
- Provide a visual checklist or schedule for your child that includes all homework assignments.
- Develop schedules and routines around homework as well as all daily tasks and activities.
- It may be helpful to "prime" your child for homework assignments prior to beginning them.
- Break down large assignments, projects, or studying for cumulative tests into component parts, and provide a checklist for each component.
- Understand teen sleep patterns and make sleep a priority.
- Have clear parental rules, lines, and limits.
- Step in when needed. But allow for mistakes.

Practicing the "I'm Sorry"

It was Saturday night. Andrew and I had just come home from a happy date night out: dinner and a movie. Our home was calm and quiet, the boys clearly already in bed. We thought we'd hear great things from the boys' twelfth-grade babysitter, Katie. Instead, it sounded like the feature presentation that played out in our home was "Boys vs. the Babysitter," and the chaos had just come to an end.

Our sweet babysitter was quiet at first. She was a bit shell-shocked, and she didn't want to get the boys in trouble, but I urged her to tell me what went down. She said that the boys had fought with each other and had gotten pretty wild. Okay, the boys do fight, and they *are* wild. They are boys. Still, their unacceptable behavior had gotten even worse. According to Katie, the boys had told her, "We won't go to bed unless you promise to bring us candy at 7:30 in the morning."

What? I couldn't believe what I was hearing. My husband wasn't happy either. There was no way this behavior was going to be taken lightly. *No way.* The next morning, we asked the boys how things went.

They didn't offer up much. So I told them that they had a delivery at the front door. They looked confused. I said, "The candy, the candy is at the front door." Nervous smiles emerged on their faces. They started to walk toward the door, both looking at the other. It was as if they couldn't believe their demands had been met. Just as they opened the door, I yelled out, "There's no candy there!" I probably shouldn't have yelled. Then I told them we needed to sit down and have a serious family meeting.

Initially, we told them they couldn't watch TV for a week, but we felt we needed to do more. We saw this as a very teachable moment. We thought about having them write her a note apologizing for their behavior, but that didn't feel completely right—they were five and six years old at the time. We also believed that they needed to understand that their behavior was inappropriate and to learn how to vocalize their regret. So instead of a note, we thought we would teach them how to *say* they were sorry. The boys had said they're sorry in our home to one another and to us, but as far as having to say they're sorry in the "real world," as it were, it thankfully hadn't been a huge issue up until that point. So we figured, "Now is the time."

With all that in mind, here's what we did: we told them that because we didn't know when we would see Katie next, we should send her a video message, and they should tell her, "We're sorry." They already loved making basketball videos of themselves dunking on the basketball hoops in their rooms and giving play-by-play accounts. I told them that just as they make basketball videos, they can make a video to say they are sorry. I told them learning to apologize to someone would help them as they grow. Luckily for all concerned, they didn't fight it. They knew I was serious about what they had done, and they knew they had to make it up to Katie. By way of instruction, I explained to them that they needed to think about what had happened the night before and how they were going to say they were sorry. It really got them to think about their actions and how they were then going to articulate an apology.

Their first video apology was a good start. Jackson, who was six, was embarrassed. He looked uncomfortable, moving his arms and legs all over the place, but he did say he was sorry. However, Asher, who was five, made it seem like he didn't know that he had been behaving inappropriately. So I had them try again, mostly for Asher in order to get him to own what he had done. This time Jackson calmed his body down and said, "I'm sorry for being mean to you. I hope you have a good day." Asher went next. In a baby voice, he said, "Katie, I'm sorry I didn't listen to you." Asher using his baby voice was an indication to me that he knew what he had done was wrong. That was the video I sent.

Katie responded within seconds: "Ahhhhh . . . so sweet. Tell the boys it's okay, and that I will see them soon." The boys read the message, then

I asked them, "How do you feel?" Asher yelled out, "Score!" When I asked what he meant, he explained that he was happy she wasn't mad at him. Jackson just smiled quietly. And after that, I didn't say anything else about it. Lesson learned in my book.

There is an ongoing conversation in our family about being kind to others. It will always be that way. I am happy to report that as the boys have grown, there haven't been any other "babysitter incidents." The boys have learned how to behave and make good choices. The necessary apologies are now mostly to each other, as sibling rivalry is alive and well in our home. The boys are so close in age and best friends. They have similar interests and enjoy being together. But they are also individuals who don't always see eye to eye. And of course, my husband and I still apologize to the boys—and to each other—for our actions, both in times of stress and in the day-to-day family dynamics that are a part of life.

A typical argument might go something like this: I'm in the kitchen cooking, and they're outside playing. I usually hear a loud yell from one of them, then another yell from the other, then both of them rush to me to give me the blow-by-blow before the other. It's just kind of their pattern. Once they get done talking, I step in and help them figure out who needs to apologize and who needs to forgive. We practice saying sorry verbally, but when things get out of control, writing can be a wonderful alternative. I'm a writer, and I enjoy it. It's how I work things out in my life. I started journaling to the boys when they were in my tummy and have been writing to them ever since. Writing works for Jackson and Asher too; we have them take a step back, head to their own rooms, and write about their feelings. Once the hot heads have cooled down, they read their notes to each other as a way to understand one another, apologize, and forgive.

I've included copies of their exact notes to each other on one occasion. The conflict was this: Asher wanted alone time in the backyard, and Jackson wanted to play with him.

Jackson's note to Asher: "Dear Asher, I don't think it's right for you to own the backyard. It is not fair and unkind. I love and want you to play, but I want to play too. When you try to exclude me, I don't like it. It makes me feel bad."

Asher's note to Jackson: "Jackson, you don't understand this part of me when I start talking that I want my alone time you said no. I want you to know that when you play catch with daddy you get more of the backyard than me and you do it a lot, so I want you to know that. O.K. That's what I want you to know."

In this instance, the boys read their notes to each other, then they both smiled and laughed. We quickly reviewed each kid's needs and settled on sharing the backyard equally. We also discussed trying to understand where each of them was coming from and how they felt about the situation. Everyone said they were sorry, and harmony was restored.

This note writing doesn't happen every time the boys have an argument. If it did, all we'd be doing is writing. But it does serve a purpose. It's just another way to practice how to say, "I'm sorry." As the boys mature, they will be more willing to see others' points of view, think about their own actions, and express their feelings and regret in a positive way.

We are our children's first teachers, and as parents we can help our kids be empathetic and express their regret. This lesson will empower them to be in touch with the world around them and their own feelings and emotions. We want them to know that although we all make mistakes sometimes, we can turn things around and learn from our experiences. We practice how to read, how to play sports, how to play an instrument, and we can practice how to say "I'm sorry" too.

Pro Parenting Tips: Practicing the "I'm Sorry"

- Practice, practice, practice. We are always learning and growing.
- Hold children accountable, but don't forget to teach them how to hold themselves accountable.
- Ask your child these questions:
  » Why do you think you behaved this way?
  » Who did you hurt?
  » How do you think your actions made him/her feel?
  » What do you need to do to avoid doing this again?
  » How can I help you?
- Model how to say, "I'm Sorry." Say sorry to your children when appropriate.
- Remember that a successful apology requires a safe space in which to say, "I'm sorry." Give your child the security to know that when they express their regret, they are heard and that the next step is moving past it. No holding grudges!
- Set realistic expectations. Let children express their regret in their own words, at a level appropriate to their age.

Practicing Kindness

Saint Teresa of Calcutta, more commonly known as Mother Teresa, has been one of my lifelong teachers, even though I have never met her, talked to her, or interviewed her. Even as a little girl growing up in a Roman Catholic family, I was able to clearly understand her message: "If you can't feed a hundred people, then feed just one." This is just one of her many teachings that have always resonated with me, and that I have lived by for most of my adult life. It opens the door to caring and kindness in a more doable or more achievable way.

I was educated in a Catholic school environment, where the curriculum taught us that to care for others just as Jesus did was paramount. It was easy to pick up habits to be helpers because we practiced it day after day, week after week, year after year. At home, I saw my parents practice this as well. They were participants in practicing kindness. They modeled kindness for our family throughout my childhood and beyond.

In my own experience, being kind toward or caring for others has always made me feel better. Based on my childhood, I think that feeling isn't why I initially want to help; rather, it's just a part of who I am now. Regardless, when I'm helping someone or after I've helped someone, I feel happy. And according to science, I'm not alone.

According to Dr. Waguih William IsHak, a professor of psychiatry at Cedars-Sinai, kindness is chemical.[41] When you are kind to another person, your brain's pleasure and reward centers light up, as if you were the recipient of the good deed—not the giver. This phenomenon is called the "helper's high." Where does this come from? Dr. IsHak explains that most research on the science of kindness is centered around the hormone oxytocin. Oxytocin has long been known as the warm, fuzzy hormone that promotes feelings of love, social bonding, and well-being, which is why it's sometimes called the love hormone. It helps form social bonds, and it's the hormone moms produce when they breastfeed in order to promote bonding with their babies. In addition to oxytocin, kindness also stimulates the production of serotonin. According to a Dartmouth study, "this feel-good chemical heals your wounds, calms you down, and makes you happy!"[42] So, with all of the benefits in mind—of either giving or receiving kindness—the question for me is this: can kindness be taught? The answer is a resounding yes.

Dr. Richard Davidson says, "It's fundamentally no different than learning how to play the violin or learning to do sports."[43] Dr. Davidson is the director of the University of Wisconsin–Madison Center for Healthy Minds. In the course of his work, he developed a mindfulness-based kindness curriculum for preschoolers to help them pay closer attention to their emotions. He says, "We found that kids who went through the kindness curriculum behaved more altruistically.[44] He also found that the kids in the kindness curriculum had a better attention span, had better grades, and showed a higher level of social competence.

I hope all this research energizes you to go out and teach your own children about kindness and caring, because kindness is considered a "soft skill," so it often doesn't get as much emphasis as academic achievement does. We know this firsthand from the results of a national survey conducted by Harvard's Making Caring Common Project, which found that a majority of youth from all kinds of backgrounds value personal success over caring for others. These children and teens report that they believe both their peers and their adult authority figures (such as teachers and parents) also value achievement over kindness.[45] What this means is that we must adjust what we are teaching to and modeling for our children, not only to promote the health benefits but also to reduce the potentially harmful academic achievement pressure that has seeped into our society. We know that children are experiencing more and more anxiety, depression, and isolation in our modern world, and the higher levels of happy hormones that result from being kind can help counteract that trend.

Here's what I decided to do about five years ago. I believed kindness should be taught as a part of the foundation of our children's development and education, so I wanted to teach this message from within the home. Because I am a teacher and a parenting journalist, I took what I was learning through my research and reporting and decided I wanted to create a program to help educate my own children—and our community—about kindness and compassion

So I founded a nonprofit called Caring Counts. The name says it all. Caring counts too. It is just as important as academics, sports, or any other extracurriculars we expose our children to. The mission of Caring Counts is to teach kindness, compassion (including self-compassion), and inclusion to kids and families, but service learning is also one big way we use our nonprofit to be kind in the world.

I believe kids can do big things. Kids are capable of great kindness if they are given the opportunity. Within our program we use our "Kind Kid Warriors" to help expand our mission of kindness through service learning. Whether it's helping build hygiene kits for the homeless or feeding food-insecure families, our kids do the hands-on work, early on in life, without waiting until the tween and teen years.

We also work with other nonprofits to promote inclusion by aiding kids with special needs. One amazing program in our community is the nonprofit West Hills Champions, founded by a mom just like me. Her sons enjoyed playing baseball, and she wanted to give them the opportunity to help kids with physical differences play baseball too. Now, each Sunday during the fall baseball season, little league baseball players come together to help the "champions"—that is, the kids with special needs—play ball.

One Sunday, some of our Kind Kid Warriors stepped in to help. My son Asher went to the field and asked the organizer to set him up with one of the champions. I'll never forget the exchange between Asher and that kid, Lucas.

After they were introduced and Asher said "hi," Lucas, who was much bigger and a year older than Asher, looked him up and down and said, "I'm going to need someone taller."

Asher looked stunned. He didn't know what to say.

The organizer laughed and said, "Lucas, you're stuck with him."

Lucas wasn't happy, but as the game progressed, the two became fast friends. Asher helped coach Lucas and cheered him on. Lucas started looking for Asher as he ran across home plate.

Do you see what is happening here? Lots of learning and growing.

Not only was Asher helping and being kind, but the exposure to the needs of others allowed Asher to see that Lucas is a kid just like him, and vice versa. Sure, there are some differences, but Asher saw him as a person with needs and wants just like himself, even though Lucas thought Asher wasn't the right fit to help him do well in baseball. Asher can really empathize with Lucas's drive because Asher always wants to win and do his best. That's what Lucas wants too. He wants to be like everyone else.

Here's another example. During the coronavirus pandemic, Caring Counts went into high gear to help one school in the LA Unified School District, providing one thousand meals and many letters of hope and love to food-insecure kids and their families in just nine weeks. And when school started in the fall of 2020, more than 2,500 school supply items were delivered. Amazingly, after the Kind Kid Warriors wrote the letters of hope and love themselves, the children and families of Lockwood Elementary wrote notes of thanks and gratitude in return. This was a full-circle moment for our Kind Kid Warriors. The kindness just keeps growing and growing. And Caring Counts is only a small nonprofit.

Now, you do not have to go out and found your own nonprofit. (Remember what Mother Teresa said.) But the point I'm making is this: modeling kind behavior is one of the most important tools you can use to get your kids to become kind, compassionate, and giving people. Debbie Goldberg, a mom of two and co-founder of Fresh Brothers Pizza, has been modeling this behavior since her children were very young. When I was thinking of starting my nonprofit, I talked to her on the phone, mom to mom, looking for insight and direction. With her permission, I'll share her answers here on how she promotes kindness and giving in her family.

Q: When did you begin introducing the concept of "giving" to your children? How old were they? And what were some of the activities that you introduced?

A: In 2004, I gave birth to boy/girl twins. I soon became president of the Beach Cities Parents of Multiples Association. They have a program called Meals on Wheels, where they ask volunteers to deliver meals to new moms of multiples. We did that often, and I'd bring the kids with me to deliver the meals. In addition, because we [my husband and I] own Fresh Brothers, a chain of pizzerias, we feel that it's crucial that we give back to our community. One Christmas, we hosted a sweatshirt collection for those in need in conjunction with a young high school student named Jason Jones. His organization is called the Sweatshirt Project, and together we collected over one thousand new and gently used sweatshirts. Our kids were five, but they helped me sort sweatshirts, move giant bags around, etc. On one Mother's Day, we collected diapers for Help A Mother Out. My kids were big helpers in that effort too!

Giving is an action. Have your children help you with whatever type of giving you are comfortable with. If you collect food for the hungry, bring your kids with you to the store, to the collection site, etc. Get them involved. Ask your kids what kind of giving and charity they'd like to be a part of. For their allowance, separate it into three jars: savings/spending/giving. Allow them to choose where their money will go to for giving. If your child loves horses, perhaps there is a horse rescue organization that you can find to give some of the money to.

Q: Can you explain how you are helping your children understand that giving is a part of life, not something that is just done during the holiday season?

A: The kids understand that we as business owners in several communities have a responsibility to give back to those communities that help our businesses thrive. When there are runs like the Manhattan Beach 10k in our town, we give out a thousand slices to the runners. We do this as a family—Mom, Dad, Nate, and Ryann. We try to involve our kids in giving opportunities as often as possible. They learn compassion and the joy of giving by living it.

You could say in a lot of ways that our business, Fresh Brothers, is our life. If you ask anyone about Fresh Brothers in our community, they will tell you that we are all about giving back to our community. It's a two-way street. . . . Every action has an equal and opposite reaction. It's thrilling to have a virtual stranger walk up to you when they see us wearing our logoed clothing and say something like "Thank you for sponsoring our baseball team," or "Thanks for all that you do for our education system." It's amazing. It never gets old!

We give because we can. We aren't wealthy. But we're blessed to have a successful business and a happy and healthy family. We realize that giving will always be a part of our lives because it's fun and we truly enjoy it.[46]

When a child begins to see others' needs beyond their own, a child is building an empathetic brain. Public health advocate Christopher Bergland puts it this way: "Because our brain's neural circuitry is malleable and can be rewired through neuroplasticity, one's tendency for empathy and compassion is never fixed. We all need to practice putting ourselves in someone else's shoes to reinforce the neural networks that allow us to 'love thy neighbor as thyself' and 'do unto others as you would have them do unto you.'"[47]

Early kindness education and the practice of empathy should be present in the home always. Just as we help nurture our children in reading and math, we must help nurture a kind and caring spirit and brain. Asher and Jackson have been helping the homeless on Skid Row in downtown Los Angeles since they were four and five years old.

Delivering Christmas presents to children in need is one of their most favorite things to do.

You can help your child walk the walk. Teach kindness early in life and empower them to take ownership of the kindness they choose to share in their home, school, and community. This gives them ownership of their service. If you're lacking ideas on how to coach them, here are some ideas to get them (and you!) started.

Pro Parenting Tips:
Ideas for Kindness for the Entire Family

- Ask elderly neighbors if they need any help.
- Regularly tell your loved ones that you love them.
- When you are served in a shop or restaurant, make eye contact, and sincerely thank the employees for their help.
- Put coins in a meter, any meter, that's about to expire.
- If you know that someone is particularly busy, offer to take their dog for a walk.
- When a thought of generosity arises within you, act on it.
- Take a friend to dinner.
- Stand up for others.
- Let someone go before you when you're standing in line.
- Compliment people on their appearance.
- Volunteer in your community.
- Stop speaking ill of others. Let your words be kind.
- Recycle.
- Think of the people in your life. What help do they need with chores or tasks?
- Don't wait to be asked.
- Be the calm voice in a stressful situation.
- Donate to your favorite charity.
- Spend some time with a senior citizen living on their own.

- Teach a child something you wish you had known at that age.
- If friends or family members are having a hard time, make sure they know that you are there for them and are available to talk and help.
- Give blood.
- Donate to or volunteer for the Make-A-Wish Foundation.
- Encourage someone to pursue their dream.
- Say "Please" and "Thank you."

Chapter 2:

Acceptance

I don't think anyone can grow unless he's
loved exactly as he is now, appreciated for what he is
rather than what he will be.
—Fred Rogers

As we move through the CASTLE Method, I am hopeful that the stories I tell illustrate how the way we parent and think about family can have either positive or negative impacts on our children, now and into adulthood. As Maya Angelou said, "Do the best you can until you know better. Then when you know better, do better."

Can you think of a time you were not accepted by a family member, a friend, a teacher, or someone else you held in high regard? It doesn't feel good, right? Now think about not being accepted by the people closest to you—your parents, the two people in the entire world who are supposed to have your back, who are supposed to see you for you, to accept all of you.

As parents, we might assume that our kids should just know that we accept them. But do we truly accept them when the going gets tough? Do we truly accept our children for being who they are and not who we think they should be? And when we do accept them, are our words and actions proving that acceptance in a way our children can recognize? It's vital to learn both how to accept our children as they are and how to show that acceptance because it turns out that feeling accepted is crucial to our development. When acceptance is not available, it can literally change our brains and our lives for the worse.

The Study of Parental Acceptance and Rejection

Being aware of the consequences of rejection and actively promoting acceptance in the home is a vital first step for truly accepting our children. Professor Emeritus of Human Development and Family Sciences at the University of Connecticut, Dr. Ronald Rohner explains that childhood experiences of warmth, affection, and other expressions of care and love "act as a buffer against many of the negative effects of rejection." What is extremely important to note are the benefits of what he calls "perceived acceptance."[48] If a child believes that his parents accept him, he can ward off more potential risk factors during childhood and into adulthood.

Dr. Rohner says, "Feelings of rejection by this very powerful person in our life [a parent] light up the same part of the brain that physical pain does. More importantly, for kids who are raised in rejecting families, it changes the structure of the brain. The brain structure and the brain function are measurably different for children who live with rejection. Regions of the brain that are essential for learning, memory, and emotional control are impacted by the rejection process. This tends to continue on through adulthood."[49] If a child perceives, even subconsciously, that her parents are rejecting her, there can be a variety of life-altering effects that extend into adulthood. The following list compiled by Dr. Rohner will help you be informed and perhaps even recognize the warning signs in your own children.[50]

Emotional Effects

- Hostility, aggression, passive aggression, or problems with management of hostility/aggression
- Impaired self-esteem
- Impaired self-adequacy
- Emotional unresponsiveness
- Emotional instability

- Negative worldview
- Dependence, or defensive independence
- Anxiety
- Insecurity
- Thought distortions

Cognitive Effects

- Disruption of early brain development associated with learning and memory
- Compromised functioning of the nervous and immune systems

Physical Effects (Often Manifest in Adulthood)

- Greater vulnerability to infections and chronic health problems such as
  » cardiovascular disease
  » chronic obstructive pulmonary disease (COPD)
  » liver disease
  » diabetes
  » stroke
  » cancer
  » asthma and allergies

It is very clear from the research that acceptance is a necessity in a child's development and well-being, both physically and mentally. With that in mind, I want to move on and share a few stories, my own and other parents', to help guide you in thinking about your own feelings of acceptance toward your children. These stories will introduce you to a wide range of what acceptance and rejection can look like and how rejecting beliefs can find their way into your parenting without you being aware of it. After that, I will then give you lots of ideas about how to accept your child for all he is. As you read, ask yourself this question: "Who is *my* kid?" Ask yourself again, "Who is she really? Who is my precious child?"

Who Is Your Kid? My Mini McEnroe

Dr. Seuss wrote, "Today you are you, that is truer than true. There is no one alive who is you-er than you." My twelve-year-old son, Asher, is competitive. He competes with his thirteen-year-old brother, Jackson, with my husband, Andrew, and with me. Yes, me! He's competitive in school, in sports, in life. It doesn't matter what it's about; he wants to win. Period.

There was an event, when he was just four, when his competitive nature appeared for all the world to see. Our family was hosting a BBQ for some of Asher's friends and their moms. Everything was going great. The boys played, the moms talked, and the "perfect" playdate was well underway. Then I had an idea: a relay race, moms versus kids. It was simple. One kid runs to another kid and tags him or her, until each kid gets a turn. Moms do the same. Fun, right? But the moms won, and then it became not fun, at least for Asher. All the kids moved on, but Asher couldn't let it go and made it known he was not happy. He told one of the moms (respectfully, at least) that the moms had cheated. He wanted a do-over. Fortunately, the moms conceded. The kids won the second time around. Asher was happy. All of the kids seemed pleased, and the gathering went on to be joyful, loud, and very long. I smiled and laughed, but I was also annoyed.

Here's another story that happened on a summer day only one year later. A tennis match in our backyard was on the calendar, and Asher and Jackson, respectively five and six at the time, were playing doubles against me, first to twenty points wins. (Sidenote: I'm not one to let my kids win all the time. I know some will debate me, but I just don't think it's the way to go. Playing for fun and learning sportsmanship are the priority for me; winning is just a bonus.) Now, I know nothing about tennis except that you hit the ball back and forth to each other. So I figured that since tennis wasn't my thing, I would play like it was a fair match-up, kind of. Jackson played calmly and kept me on my toes. But Asher would boil every single time I won a point. He yelled at me, "You just want to win, Mommy, and it's not fair!" But whenever they scored a point, Asher would jump for joy, exclaiming, "You're going down!" As a reminder, the kid was *five*.

Eventually, I had nineteen points, just one point away from victory. There were three takeovers as both boys decided there was some sort of issue with my points, but finally, I made it to twenty. Then the explosion arrived.

Asher screamed at the top of his lungs, "It's not fair! You cheated!" He flung his new tennis racket to the ground and threw the ball, at his top strength, right at me! Yikes! And there was no calming him down. He just couldn't take the loss.

Asher has been this way his entire life. He reminds me of a mini John McEnroe. Many of us who are tennis fans have seen the tennis great at his worst on the court. Fortunately, Asher's reaction to losing that tennis match is the most extreme response he has had so far, but in everything he does, he sees competition and believes that he *must* win at all costs. Back then, Jackson offered him a re-match and we were finally able to console him, but the effort that went into his temper tantrum was tough to watch. As his mom, I didn't want him to tense up and feel bad. What parent does? I want him to be happy, have fun, and enjoy the game. So after that, I had to admit that I had to figure out how to manage Asher's "passion" and competitiveness without squashing what I have always genuinely believed is a positive trait which will serve him well in life: being driven.

And so, *this* process marches on. Asher is still my mini McEnroe, but time and maturity and an ongoing awareness of his needs have helped him move forward in a positive way. Don't get me wrong; the kid still wants to win at everything. And I do mean everything. For example, in the first, second, and third grades, he insisted that he get perfect scores on his spelling tests each week. In those three years, he was able to get every single spelling word correct except for one: "each." (That's after having spelled "appendicitis" with no problem.) But thankfully he was okay with the mistake. This is progress; he is channeling his competitive spirit toward good grades and learning to accept less than 100 percent.

At the time of writing, Asher is eleven, and he is still a very strong spirit. He's been this way as long as he's been on the planet. It can be very hard to manage at times, but I wouldn't have it any other way. This is what makes Asher *my* Asher.

So how can you help children who might be fiercely competitive or who find it difficult to regulate their emotions in certain situations? As parents we have to allow our children to be who they are, but also channel those strong emotions in a healthy and positive way. We can't just say, "Stop that. It's inappropriate." We have to take the time to help our children lean into their emotions, even the ugly ones. Allowing kids to feel those emotions, giving them the space to understand the "why" of their emotions, and then helping them move on to more positive emotions—doing all this is a great way to show your child that you accept him, to tell him, "I don't want to control you. I want to help you be you, but in a way that is healthy."

Who Is Your Kid? My Kid Is Transgender

Acceptance is the key to understanding, love, and unconditional care. Before we move on to another family's journey, I want to state something clearly: all youth need acceptance. Unfortunately, in our country, not all youth are accepted: lesbian, gay, bisexual, and transgender youth are suffering rejection at rates that are inconceivable. My goal in this section is to provide resources to educate parents who have LGBTQ children so that you can develop better understanding and acceptance.

Parental acceptance for LGBTQ youth is especially vital when society outside the home trends toward rejection. Government and other societal action in the United States have often increased the stigma and isolation many transgender youth feel. Pediatrician

Gayathri Chelvakumar and gender development educator Scott F. Leibowitz have observed just such a trend in Ohio: "Transgender youth already experience higher levels of stigma, bullying and discrimination compared to their cisgender peers. These experiences are associated with significantly higher rates of negative mental health outcomes, including, tragically, markedly higher rates of suicidality. During a time when the world is collectively enduring the trauma of a changed society from the COVID-19 pandemic, the last thing that transgender youth need are lawmakers restricting their athletic participation or eliminating important beneficial medical options for them."[51]

Keeping this trend in mind, I want to tell you the story of a mother who faced an extraordinary realization about who her child is. It wasn't an easy path nor what most parents will ever encounter. When her child was in seventh grade, this mom found out from another parent that her child identifies as male, which is not the gender he was assigned at birth. In other words, her child is transgender, something she hadn't known for the first decade of his life. Take that in. Imagine the confusion for this mother.

She didn't handle the news perfectly at first. In her own words, "I was like, 'Wait, what?' And I went to go talk to him, and he was very upset that I had been told that [he was transgender]. And [he] felt very, kind of attacked. My reaction wasn't angry, but he felt the energy coming off me, which was like, 'I'm not comfortable with this.' I wasn't embracing where he was at all. I was really, really struggling, and I did that for a year. I wasn't going to ask him about it, because I just wanted to see if it would go away on its own."[52]

If it's not clear already, that's the wrong approach to take. LGBTQ children cannot afford to feel rejected or ignored at home. For some, home may be the only refuge they have. The GLSEN 2019 National School Climate Survey shows that schools are not safe for LGBTQ students. Almost all the respondents, 98.8 percent, had heard "gay" in a negative way at school. Of those, 75.6 percent heard these types of remarks frequently, and 91.8 percent reported that they felt distressed after hearing this language.[53] GLSEN, the Gay, Lesbian & Straight Education Network, is the leading national education organization focused on ensuring safe schools for all students. If you are a parent of an LGBTQ child, or even if you aren't, I encourage you to take advantage of the resources GLSEN provides (available on their website, www.glsen.org) to educate yourself and find ways to support LGBTQ youth in schools and at home.[54]

According to the National Center for Biotechnology Information (NCBI), LGBTQ youth who perceive strong support from their families tend to have better mental health and lower risk of drug or alcohol abuse. But "the influence of parenting practices on health is more complex for LGBTQ youth compared with cisgender heterosexual youth, as the success of these strategies requires that parents are aware of, and at a minimum tolerate, their child's LGBTQ identity and/or gender expression and provide accurate health information tailored to their needs."[55] In other words, supportive and accepting parents who use open, mutual, and low-conflict communication can provide their children with better care.

You may think that the story I shared about the mother and her transgender teen is a unique situation, but according to a 2019 CDC report, the public transgender youth population is growing, and transgender youth exist in much greater numbers than researchers had previously estimated. LGBTQ youth are here, and rejection of their identities can have dire consequences. In fact, the report shows that almost 2 percent of high school students identify as transgender, and sadly, 35 percent of them attempted suicide in 2017.[56]

Luckily, this mother and son had a happier journey. She said that acknowledging her child's needs and then accepting him for who he is allowed her to have a deep and loving relationship with him. "I think the most surprising thing for me is how much better we're all doing after we stopped fighting it. It's so much easier than it was. And I think if I had known that it would have been a little easier. You know, to kind of go with the flow."[57]

What a beautiful and inspiring message from this mother. She finally saw who her child really was, and she loved him unconditionally. She accepted him, and she showed that acceptance in word and deed. This is what our children need and want from us. It doesn't matter if it makes us uncomfortable as parents. We must honor our children; we have to accept them for who they are, as the human beings they were created to be.

Suzanne Morris says, "Unconditional love is the first thing a parent has for a child, knowing that you are loved no matter what."[58] The link between acceptance and unconditional love is obvious, even though they can feel quite different. Acceptance is something we must practice in our parenting, while unconditional love comes much more naturally. I'll talk more about love and how Morris describes a child's "Birthrights" in chapter 5, but for now, keep these words from Dr. Rohner in mind: "Parental love is the single most important factor in a child's life."[59]

Who Is Your Kid? My Kid with Special Needs

Now I want to dig into another specific group of children in our world: kids with special needs. During the 2019–2020 school year, 14.4 percent of all students in the United States between the ages of three and twenty-one were special education students. To illustrate the importance of accepting our kids with special needs, I want to offer up one more story, a painful and catastrophic one.

Lawyer Georgianna Kelman calls herself "The Special Kids' Attorney." At birth, her son, Brandon was diagnosed with what she explained to me as a "massive malformation in his brain." She and her husband were told that Brandon would never walk or talk.[60] She said, "I didn't think for a minute that my life would take the turn that it did. I thought my life was going to be perfect." She now calls this turn in her life her "fairytale revised."

"I always describe it as a death," she says. "You've got to mourn that expectation of a child and the life that you envisioned for yourself. You must come to terms with that and abandon that. I have families [who I work with] that are trying to fit a square peg into a round hole."

Of course, parents will do all they can to aid in their child's development, with therapies and anything else the medical field can offer. But Kelman says that eventually "you have to accept who your child is, the parts of your child that you're never going to be able to change. Obviously [you] implement everything you can, in terms of supports, services, school, and all of these things that you can do, but [you have to] know your child will never be this picture-perfect child." You must fully embrace who your child is. Special needs and atypical development are part of who your kid is. Of course, doing this isn't easy. Even Kelman struggled. The whole family struggled and continues to struggle.

Brandon has made a lot of progress, but obstacles still continue to arise. He has been in the Los Angeles Unified School District full-inclusion program since kindergarten. At the time of writing, he is now a senior at Birmingham High School. He has exceeded all expectations, and while he is still limited, he can walk and talk, and his life is full. He is the manager of the basketball team at Birmingham. But he can't play his favorite sport, and it's extremely hard for him to make friends, even with all the support from his mom, dad, brothers, school, and community. He is not completely alone in that as a teen, but it has been painful for his mother to watch (a feeling that I think speaks to every single person on the planet).

Kelman told me how she had always tried to find opportunities for Brandon to make friends. One year, she found out about a basketball event which other special needs kids would be attending. She asked Brandon if he'd like to go, and he said yes. "It was basketball players hanging out with severely disabled kids," she told me, "and Brandon got assigned one basketball player, and they got to hang out for a little bit. Then the kids began to separate." She saw Brandon was upset. He asked her if they could leave. She said yes but asked what was wrong.

He didn't immediately answer, but on the way home, he said, in a loud and clear voice, something Kelman said she'll never forget: "Why do you have to advertise my disability for people to want to be my friend? Why do I have to keep telling people I am disabled? Why can't they just be my friend? Why can't regular people just be my friends? Why do people have to feel sorry for me to be my friend? I'm tired of telling people that I am disabled."

She told him, "My God, you are right. You are right."

"Stop bringing me to these groups with kids with disabilities. I just want to be included without the group," Brandon told her.

And she listened. She really listened. "This was such a light-bulb moment in my head. . . . He told me this, and I never thought for a second this would hurt him. My whole mission is inclusion. But he told me otherwise, and now I understand more. I will honor his request."

Even with all her effort, she saw she couldn't change him and how he felt. She really had to see Brandon for Brandon.

Kelman offered up this story to really prove the point that we have to see and hear our children for exactly who they are: "Really, really listen to your kid. He will tell you who he is."

The bottom line is that we all know the parents who wish their child was a straight-A student or the best athlete on campus when she's not. And those wishes just aren't fair to our children. We must adore and cherish our children for who they are—all of them—not just the parts that make us proud but the parts that make us uncomfortable as well. We must develop acceptance and unconditional love to truly allow our children to be who they are and who they are meant to be.

Help Your Children Feel Your Acceptance

Remember the term "perceived acceptance"? Once you've figured out how to accept all of your child, whoever he is, it's just as important to figure out how to let your child feel your acceptance. Here are some ideas to get you started.

As a reporter, I am a person who is tasked with really listening and trying to understand people and situations. I have come to learn this skill is quite useful in parenting. Listening—really listening to what our children are saying to us—is how we can really get to know who they are. Start with listening. It's going to look very different for every kid. You'll be taking a great first step by starting to figure out how to get your child to talk to you. Asher, my mini McEnroe, talks to me when I play with him. He opens up on the basketball court or when we're playing chase. When you find that space for your kid, she will tell you who she is.

Next, empower your children to be themselves. Acknowledge who your kids are by watching them and supporting them with affirmations and questions that express curiosity:

- "Wow, I love how you are being you."
- "You are making very good choices for yourself."
- "What matters to you right now?"

Embrace who your child is without trying to change him. Learn his goals and help him be the best version of himself. Ask yourself thoughtfully, "Who is my kid?"

After conflicts or stress, talk about feelings. When your child is struggling, take the time to talk to her. Tell her you understand the frustration she's feeling, then ask her to explain any other feelings she's having. Ask questions like "Did you feel sad, or mad, or something else?" and "How can I help you?" Practice this type of discussion in the home as often as possible so that your children become accustomed to it. Be patient and be positive. As a former teacher, I've learned that it's important to point out to your child that each one of us will learn who we are at our own pace. You can tell your child to be patient with herself as she grows into the person she is meant to be.

Teach your child to love and adore himself, even when he feels like he doesn't deserve it. Self-compassion will help your child accept and love himself. Accept your child unconditionally. And when you don't, acknowledge the mistake and tell him you'll do better next time.

> ## Pro Parenting Tips: Toss Out Preconceived Notions and Just Accept
> - When conflict is brewing, stop, breathe, and just accept your child for all that he is, and everything he's not.
> - Be brave and know your child is where she is supposed to be in this moment. You don't have to try to fix things.
> - Begin with compassion and unconditional love, and then see where it takes you.

Teaching Your Child Self-Acceptance

No one ever believes me when I say that I am a very shy, socially awkward person, but it's true. It's part of who I am. Just ask my husband, who I command each time we walk into a party or event to *"not leave me alone."*

Now, after many years, I can talk about my anxiety easily, if I've warmed up to you and feel comfortable in the moment. When I do, the shock and disbelief quickly follow. Next, the questions come:

"How on earth then can you be a TV reporter?"

"What are you talking about? I would have never thought such a thing!"

"You're joking, right?"

Wrong. So here's where the connection to parenting comes in: How do I, a grown woman who herself struggles with self-acceptance, help my child move more easily through life than I have? How can I help my child build a stronger foundation in self-acceptance? As ever, let's start with the research.

Self-Acceptance in the Education and Counseling of Young People

Can you imagine a world where critics or bullies couldn't strip away your child's own self-love? Not that your child wouldn't encounter these people or experiences, but that when she did, she could stand proudly, secure and filled with self-love and compassion for herself? How can we change how our children see themselves? If we can nurture our children toward self-love and acceptance in life, their world can be whatever they choose it to be.

Sabine Beecher discusses how self-acceptance involves detaching our self-appraisal from what others think: "Self-acceptance is acknowledging yourself and recognizing that everything about you is a fact. That fact is your starting point and you go on from there. With self-acceptance you can look at yourself and say, 'There is this part of me (my nose) that I don't like. There is that trait of mine (I get impatient) that I hate. I acknowledge that they are all part of me.' There are no conditions. . . . Self-acceptance is your inner security."[61]

And with that security comes the ability to build resilience as well as better mental health and well-being. Resilience is the capacity to recover from difficulties, a kind of mental toughness that allows children to bounce back from disappointment and look for another, better way. If a child is resilient, failure and disappointment will not be disastrous. According to a 2009 study, "promoting self-acceptance in early childhood can also serve as a protective or preventative factor in the development of future mental health problems. Both parents and teachers can teach and encourage the practice of self-acceptance within the child's environment. Therefore, it is important that self-acceptance be taught and promoted in early childhood education."[62]

Remember that children's brains are constantly under construction. This means that they are malleable and can learn very early in life. The evidence is growing that even three- and four-year-olds can begin to develop a resilient spirit and a sense of confidence. And so, you can start to teach your child to be self-accepting beginning during the toddler years. And you don't have to do it alone, either. In some schools, curriculums are now targeting self-acceptance, also often called "self-awareness," in young children. Children are taught the idea of self-acceptance through lessons that may involve stories, activities, or content that illustrates how one can practice self-acceptance. I made use of that resource myself when Jackson was in preschool. I keep journals for each of my kids. Here's one of the entries from that time:

September 6, 2011

Dear Jackson,

You are now in preschool, and some days you can't wait to jump out of the car. But other days, you simply refuse to get out. Today, it was rough, but you gave me a hint on how to help. You said to me, with tears running down your face, "Mommy, I am shy to make friends."

When Jackson told me this, I understood his feelings to my core. I wanted so much to walk into that preschool and help Jackson fight his fears and watch him play and be joyful. I wanted to offer a play date to a kid I thought might be the right fit for a friend. But I pulled myself back. And I did it with the help of Jackson's preschool teacher, Ms. Anissa. Instead of me fixing it for Jackson, his teacher asked him to do two things: First, she asked him to ask a kid that he wanted to be friends with for a play date. Surprisingly, he was up for the task and did just that. Second, she suggested he draw a picture that would represent a happy day at school with lots of friends all around him. This picture would then be laminated for him to look at in the car on the way to school each day.

I remember how proud Jackson was after he showed me the picture. It still means a lot to me when I look at it. I can remember how tough it was for him at the time. I can remember that some days the picture worked, and some days it did not. I wanted so much to help him then, but I knew I needed to let him help himself. This knowledge did not come from an inner feeling or some epiphany; in fact, I had to fight the urge to just fix the problem for him. Rather, this understanding came from the most wonderful preschool director and teachers I was so blessed to know. Ms. Anissa knew just what to do to help him help himself.

It was no accident that I found myself at this precious school. I had searched long and hard for the best preschool for my kids. I will tell you all I know about picking the perfect preschool for your child in chapter 7, but all I'll say now is that Jackson's preschool built their program around the Montessori Method. Its founder, Maria Montessori, once said, "The most important period of life is not the age of university studies, but the first one, the period from birth to the age of six."[63] As I watched Jackson grow during that time, the truth of that statement was proven to me.

Today, Jackson is still that very sweet, sometimes shy, sensitive kid. He is in seventh grade and has lots of friends. Maturation helps with that, but I often think back to that picture he drew, and I can see in that smile he drew for his own face that he was accepting who he was. He was making the world a more comfortable place for him to be in. He had a hand in fixing what he could fix, all by himself, at age three, and that feeling of empowerment stayed with him. Even during COVID-19, his self-acceptance is stronger than ever. Here's an article I wrote for *Your Teen Magazine* showcasing his growth.[64]

My Son Course Corrected— and Rediscovered His Love of Golf

Last year, my twelve-year-old son, Jackson, was set for his final season at Encino Little League. He was looking forward to making the All-Star team, just like he had every season, and heading to Cooperstown to culminate his little league experience. But then the pandemic hit, and his life was turned upside down like the rest of us.

Jackson has played baseball since he was three years old. He loves it, but the pandemic meant he had to put his passion on hold. With baseball on hold, Jackson took up golf, one of the only safe social distancing sports a kid can play. His dad loves the sport and has played it for years, and it wasn't long before Jackson caught the bug too.

Jackson started taking lessons and found the coach of his dreams. James was the perfect fit for Jackson, the patient, talented coach every parent wants for their athlete. Jackson wanted lessons every week and then, when tournament play came back with pandemic guidelines, he was ready to compete. As a new kid golfer, he had to start on the Southern California PGA Junior Developmental Tour, known as JDT. It gave him the opportunity to learn how to play in a tournament, get used to competing, and develop as a golfer.

Because Jackson is a competitor and always reaching for more, he quickly decided he wanted to move up to the next tour, the Southern California PGA Players Tour, and play 18-hole tournaments with more experienced and stronger players. To move up, a golfer must play at least three JDT tournaments and score a maximum of a 7 over par. Jackson reached his first golf goal and was ready to compete with better golfers. Or so he thought.

Playing golf, which had brought him so much joy, became frustrating, exhausting, and not fun. He was struggling and beginning to lose his confidence—and his love of the game. After a few rough months, Jackson decided and wanted to talk it out with my husband and me. I thought he was going to say he wanted to stop playing golf, at least for a while. Instead, he asked if he could move back down to the Junior

Developmental Tour.

Our highly competitive kid figured out what he needed to do to "get his joy back." Jackson went on to tell us he felt like he needed more time on the developmental tour and wanted to know what it felt like to win a tournament. He was reaching for the feeling of joy he had experienced with his earlier accomplishments. He didn't care what anyone else thought of his step back. For him, it wasn't about failure and not being good enough—he wanted to follow his heart to what would make him feel joy for the game again.

Since Jackson rejoined the lower level JDT, he has won three tournaments and has been in the mix for a top three finish in almost every event. He still plays on the developmental tour but has now expanded to play US Kids Golf tournaments, where he plays eighteen holes and his best golf buddy in the world, Dad, caddies for him. So, while he continues to develop his skills, he's beginning to stretch more too.

What I learned from this experience is that by giving my son the ability to move through activities freely, and to course correct on his own when needed, he learned to follow his heart. How he got there doesn't matter. He got on the path, listened to his instincts, and found his way to what would make him happiest. He's learning to trust himself. And as he grows, I know he's learning to find his way, and his joy, no matter where life takes him.

Boys Book Club

Jackson's journey during that period is one example of how self-acceptance grows resilience and so much more. Now I want to share another real-life example of how young kids can build their self-acceptance and resiliency and learn how to move in the world successfully as they grow and develop. This story also shows how you can help as parents.

Reading, as we all know, is one of the basic foundations for learning. If we can develop confident readers at an early age, children will enjoy school more and have more success. We all learn to read at our own pace, but as a former elementary school teacher, I knew how important it was to make reading fun and engaging for my kids early on. So when my boys began kindergarten, I decided to start a "Boys Book Club." Sound a bit young for five-year-olds? Maybe not.

There were eight boys in Asher's kindergarten class, and we invited all eight to participate in the book club. Everyone signed up instantly. Asher, as host for the first book club, picked out the book, one about puppies. It was a chapter book, which is challenging, but that's what he wanted. He wanted it because we had just gotten a puppy of our own, Addison. It meant something to him; it was something he could engage in and connect with. Again, fun and engagement are vital at this stage, so I allowed it.

I soon got exasperated emails and calls from the other moms in the club, stating that the book was too hard for some of the boys, though two had no problem with it. (That's how it goes with early readers; they're all over the map.) I quickly sent back positive messages encouraging moms to read along with their little guys or to simply read it to them if it was just too advanced. After all, reading is reading. Kids learn to read whether people read to them or with them. To all the parents' credit, they eventually accepted where their children were in their individual reading journeys and went for it.

Once things were settled, and enough time passed to ensure everyone was able to read the book, we planned our first meeting. I assisted Asher in coming up with questions for his friends so they could discuss the book. I will say that this group of kids was exceptional in that they all participated happily in the discussion. There was even some talking over each other as excitement ensued—*It's working!* I thought. *They're excited!*—but for the most part we all participated in the discussion, boys and moms, and after a while they went into regular boy-mode. And a wild soccer game topped off the meeting.

We continued with our book club through the first and second grades. Some of the book selections were big hits; others were not. We lost a couple who decided it wasn't for them after a while, but we quickly recruited two others to round off the group.

Now here's where it gets interesting. In June of the boys' second-grade year, one of the boys hosted the final book club of the school year. They had been in it for three years at that point, and the routine was established. Before the meeting began, the parents were all inside, talking, eating, and drinking wine—another positive point for the book club, at least for the parents. The boys were busy playing a very strenuous game of what looked like rugby. When I walked outside, the host mom said, "Okay guys, time to get the meeting started. You can go back to your game afterward."

The boys quickly gathered on the patio, I sat on a bench off to the side, and the host mom was called away to help a younger sibling grab something to drink. That's when the magic happened.

The boy who hosted the book club stood on top of a table (because that's what boys do) and called order to the meeting. He had his paper filled with questions in hand. He had written every question himself— with no help from Mom or Dad, his father reported later. The kid went on to tell everyone which order they would be answering the questions. Everyone had a number: first, second, third, etc. Everyone seemed to agree with the instructions, and off they went, question and answer after question and answer, everyone participating, everyone laughing, everyone talking.

Usually I'm the type of mom who likes to get in on the discussion, but this time something was different. A handful of the parents never even made it out to the patio to watch or participate, and the few that were outside were busy talking about summer camp sign-ups and paying little attention to the discussion.

So the boys just held their own meeting. They discussed the book and loudly shouted their differing opinions. And not one parent participated, not once. These boys were now seven and eight years old. Do you see what is happening here? As the research states, it's vital to provide kids with the space to develop and practice self-acceptance outside of the classroom. As the boys ran their own book club independent of their parents, they were building self-acceptance. They didn't need us there (except perhaps to give them a ride home). They did it all on their own. It was amazing.

These little guys now know that their opinions matter in the world, that they can participate in a meeting run by them and for them, that they can be confident in public speaking outside of school and accept themselves as they are. Most importantly, they learned to accept each other and the process—again, *outside* of the classroom, where no one cared who the best reader was, or who was the most articulate. As a former kindergarten teacher, I knew the boys were likely to have varying levels of reading fluency and might have self-doubt, concern, maybe anxiety about reading. It was a skill they were only just beginning to practice. But no one cared. They simply accepted each other and felt safe in return. The benefits go on and on and on. I loved seeing what I saw!

As I write this today, seven years later, all the boys are now in sixth grade, and the book club is still going strong. Hooray for these kids' commitment to the book club!

Pro Parenting Tips: Teaching Self-Acceptance

- Define terms like "self-acceptance" and "resilience." Once your kids know what the words mean, you will be able to use them at vital teaching points.
- Practice self-acceptance daily. Model it for your kids by using phrases like "I'm learning and growing. I'll be just fine."

- Teach resilience early. Let toddlers do age-appropriate tasks like washing their body with a washcloth during bath time under your supervision.
- Talk to a child at the child's level. When she says, "I can't ride a bike," or "I can't read," say, "You're right that you don't yet know how to ride a bike, but you're learning. Be patient with yourself."
- Teach your child to talk to you. Look into his eyes and listen to his concerns, so he knows that what he says matters to you.
- If a child makes a mistake, step back when you can and allow her to fix what she's able to for herself. Then praise her and allow her to be proud of her accomplishments.
- Surround your family with smart, capable teachers, friends, and parents. People who love, care for, and can see your child for who they are can shape the child you love so much for the better.
- Model empathy. Offer up a story from your own childhood that relates to your child's situation and shows him he's not the only person who feels this way.
- Allow for lots of mistakes as your child builds resilience. Help your child understand that there's no race to be run and that she will have your love and acceptance regardless of how many mistakes she makes.
- Read and watch TV together. Find underdogs in books and on the screen who practice resilience and hard work and help your children to identify and empathize with them. Here are a few great picture books to start with: *Oh, the Places You'll Go!* by Dr. Seuss, *The Name Jar* by Yangsook Choi, and *Princesses Are Not Perfect* by Kate Lum.

Caring for Mental Health, Starting Now

As we continue to grow our children's self-acceptance, it is important to focus on mental and physical health in addition to emotional resilience. On the physical health side, much of the work is already being done. As parents and educators, we talk to our kids in the preschool years about safety and physical health. We educate them about being the "boss of their bodies" (that from author and teacher Pattie Fitzgerald[65]). We give them the age-appropriate language to normalize and talk about their private parts: "penis" vs. "pee pee." We talk incessantly about their physical health, providing them with nutrition and fitness education.

But when it comes to mental health, our children—especially those twelve years old and younger—are often left to fend for themselves, as are their parents. By the time our kids enter the tween and teen years, we are primed to react to the mental health issues they display, but many problems can be prevented if parents start earlier. We need to change the paradigm and focus just as much on our preschoolers, kindergarteners, and first through fifth graders. We must proactively teach them how to take care of their mental health and well-being as if their lives depended on it. We must teach our children positive self-affirmations and help them avoid harmful ideas, language, and actions. Because if you look at the statistics, there's no more time to waste.

Kids' Mental Health

According to a recent report from the CDC, beginning in April 2020, the proportion of children's mental health–related visits compared to regular visits increased by 24 percent for children ages five to eleven and 31 percent for children ages twelve to seventeen compared to those in 2019 and remained elevated through October 2020.[66] Of course, this trend does reflect the trauma we have all felt due to the pandemic. But if you look at where we were before COVID-19 hit us, our kids were already suffering from bullying, unhealthy social media exposure, and academic achievement pressure. Here's an even more troubling statistic: the rate of suicide for people ages ten to twenty-four increased nearly 60 percent between 2007 and 2018. Suicide is the second leading cause of death for ten- to thirty-four-year-olds per the CDC.[67]

If we are going to get ahead of this disturbing trend, we must be proactive and think bigger. Dealing with your child's legitimate mental health problems can be exhausting, scary, and challenging. So why wouldn't we look at where we are and start to rethink mental health education and preventative work before those problems arise? Here's how to begin doing that:

- First, we must be explicit in our discussions about mental health and well-being. We must tell our children clearly and often that mental health is just as important as physical health and safety.
- Second, we can teach children under twelve strategies for better mental health. We can advocate to help parents and teachers via teacher training and parent education to learn how to implement these techniques in the home and in schools. We can use books and school curriculums to educate kids, parents, and families.
- Third, as the adults in our children's lives, we must model self-love and self-compassion. We know from research that we can grow empathy, compassion, and love. When you learn to love yourself, you can better take care of yourself, not just physically but mentally as well. Your children will look to you and learn.

All this may seem like an enormous, even exhausting task. But we really have no other choice. We must change the way we think about kids' mental health, our approach, and the education around it. However, you don't have to tackle all the possible problems at once. I certainly can't cover it all in this book, let alone this chapter. Instead, I'll explore one possible mental health issue that you can counter using these steps—starting right now.

As I said at the start of this section, we often address physical health issues automatically with our children. Diet and exercise are two of the most prominent areas. However, the way our society approaches physical health issues like weight and diet can often give rise to mental health issues, creating one problem in the process of solving another. Now, I'm not saying that we don't need to be aware of what our children eat and whether they exercise. We *absolutely do*. What I want to do here is educate you about how to approach your children's nutrition and fitness in a way that defends mental health much as it does physical health.

Pro Parenting Tips: Strategies toward Better Mental Health in Children

- Manage emotions, both yours and your child's. Identify the emotion, understand the emotion, feel the emotion, and then move on to a more positive emotion, if possible. Walk your child through these steps by asking thoughtful questions and modeling possible answers.
- Use deep breathing and mindfulness techniques to help your child regain calm.
- Have your children record their thoughts and experiences. Older children can keep a journal, while younger ones can draw pictures or write simple sentences with your help.
- Incorporate mental health discussions into your everyday life. Talk about your own mental health as much as you ask your children about theirs.
- Educate yourself on mental wellness. Read books and articles and watch videos and documentaries. There is a wealth of information out there ready and waiting for you to look for it.

- Utilize professional mental health services. Licensed therapists have expertise beyond what you can manage as a parent. Let them be a resource for you and your child.

Nutrition and Fitness: Defending Mental and Physical Health

Most of the mental health obstacles we run into regarding physical health arise from legitimate concerns about the real dilemmas of nutrition and fitness in today's world. Once you understand that those dilemmas have solutions, it will be easier for you to talk to your kids about them in ways that preserve their mental health. So before I get into the mental side of things, let's talk about diet.

I don't know about you, but before I was a mother, I wasn't very interested in sugar intake or the best nutritional diet. I was a busy college student who would eat on the run. After that, I was a working reporter who ate on the road all of the time. I ate the food I could get and gobble down the fastest in between interviews, writing, and live shots. Basically, I was constantly eating the worst junk available.

Enter my kids. Of course, we all know in our heads that kids need fruits, vegetables, and some source of protein, but it's hard to actually put that knowledge into practice—and it's getting harder all the time. When it came to all those packaged foods, even the supposedly healthy choices, I was incredibly confused. And I'm not alone. Nearly 59 percent of consumers have a hard time understanding nutrition labels.[68] I tried to eat together with my children at home as much as possible, so I could at least watch what was going into their bodies. Still, what I brought home and what we ate outside of the home wasn't always the best, and I knew it. I needed some serious help.

Obesity in Children

There are excellent reasons why we as parents should be concerned with monitoring our children's diets. Case in point, the percentage of children with obesity in the United States has more than tripled since the 1970s. Today, about 17 percent of children are overweight or obese.[69] That trend has no doubt inspired real worries for many parents, with legitimate cause. In addition to long-term health problems such as heart disease, type 2 diabetes, and cancer, childhood obesity can also cause "more immediate health risks," such as breathing problems like asthma and sleep apnea, joint problems, and musculoskeletal discomfort. There are even mental health risks, such as anxiety, depression, and low self-esteem.[70] And now we know that obesity also affects brain development.

A study funded by the National Institute of Health followed 10,000 teens over a ten-year period, analyzing results from 3,190 nine- and ten-year-olds in 2017. The study found that obese children tended to have a thinner prefrontal cortex, the part of the brain that controls memory, planning, and decision making.[71] Since the most important time for brain development is childhood, this finding is not something to be taken lightly. So what can parents do about it?

To begin with, it's important to distinguish between added sugar and naturally occurring sugars. Ironically, there's no sugarcoating the fact that sugar is a problem. Did you know that the average American consumes eighty-eight grams of added sugar a day? That is as much as seven times more than the daily recommended amount. In one sense, this trend simplifies things a great deal. Reducing the amount of added sugar in your child's diet is one of the quickest and easiest ways to improve overall physical health and well-being. For example, many people who reduce the amount of added sugar in their diets report improved moods, increased weight loss, and decreased fatigue.

Fruits, dairy products, and some vegetables already have sugar before processing. We call these "naturally occurring sugars." In all processed foods (soda, candy, cereal, etc.), it's safe to say that most sugar has been "added." And where does this leave our children? Unfortunately, beginning with breakfast, the cereals in our stores are packed with more sugar than desserts. In some cases, these cereals have up to twenty grams of added sugar in one serving.

According to the American Heart Association, children should have no more than twenty-five grams (or six teaspoons) of added sugar per day. So how do you implement this in real life, day in and day out? Only twenty-five grams. With how pervasive added sugar is, limiting the amount is not easy. At least for me, it's one of the hardest things to achieve as a parent. But in today's world, we have to try, and a great starting point is to teach our children to think about and understand what they are putting into their bodies.

In 2012, I got a crash course in healthy eating when I interviewed registered dietitian and nutritionist Melissa Hooper, who deals specifically with childhood obesity. (In addition to the advice I'll share here, feel free to check out her website: https://www.bite-sizenutrition.com.)

To begin with, it's imperative to educate our children from the beginning, so they can take ownership of their eating habits and physical activity. Melissa Hooper suggests that you ask your children questions like "How many grams of added sugar are you supposed to have today? How many grams do you think you've had today?" Questions allow a child to think about his health without feeling that you as a parent are prejudging him.

When you go shopping, children can pick out items. As soon as you see what they've picked, tell them, "Please read for me how many grams of added sugar is in that box. How many grams are there per serving?" Because of Hooper's advice, I have been doing this since Jackson and Asher were three and four. Now, it's just as ingrained for them as brushing your teeth in the morning and at night. It's just what we do: we read labels. It gives them a sense of ownership and responsibility for their own physical health.

If you're reading this and thinking, "Come on, how in the heck can your kids only take in twenty-five grams of added sugar per day?" just know that *you are not alone.* This is an almost impossible task because of the way most of our food is made and packaged now. In my family, we still haven't cracked the code on how to eat *only* twenty-five grams of added sugar per day, every day. But we are much more aware of what we are putting into our bodies. And we do it without measuring and weighing everything we eat. This helps us to concentrate on building healthy habits instead of overfocusing on raw numbers. According to Hooper, "It's not about this strict twenty-five-gram policy. It's about knowledge and being able to make healthier choices in the world we live in. It's about finding ways to enjoy, just not in excess."

Here I want to add a note about eating disorders. We live in a society that encourages obsessing about physical image. This pressure can increase the risks of your child developing an eating disorder. Here are the facts from Johns Hopkins All Children's Hospital (see their website for more information and resources):

- Thirty million people in the United States have an eating disorder.
- Ninety-five percent of people with eating disorders are between the ages of twelve and twenty-five.
- Eating disorders have the *highest* risk of death of any mental illness.
- Eating disorders affect all genders, all races, and every ethnic group.
- Genetics, environmental factors, and personality traits all contribute to the risk of developing an eating disorder.[72]

Dr. Sarah Stromberg, from Johns Hopkins All Children's Hospital, said the following: "It is important to remember that eating disorders are both medical and mental health disorders, so it is incredibly difficult for children/teens to recover on their own. They need treatment and consistent support from their families. This means parents should not be afraid to closely monitor their child or teen's eating behaviors. Parents should be ensuring their child is eating a variety of foods and obtaining adequate nutrition each day."[73]

As you work to build good habits of nutrition and fitness in your home, remember that a balanced approach to teaching is beneficial to shaping young kids, teens, and emerging adults. You as a parent can decrease the risks by reminding your child that he is beautiful even if his natural weight isn't similar to that of the kids around him.

It may help you to remember that some children will naturally weigh more than others regardless of diet and exercise. Childhood obesity is influenced by many factors besides diet, including genetics, metabolism—that is, how your body changes food and oxygen into energy—exercise, environmental factors, and social and individual psychology. It's important not to be fixated on getting your child to a specific number of pounds. So work with your family physician to figure out what a healthy weight is for your specific child and what balance of factors will help get her there.

Here's some more practical advice. For one, talk about eating food for enjoyment. As an Italian mama, I see food as an important part of our culture. "Mangia!" ("Eat!" in Italian) is a word often used in our home. And I certainly don't want to deprive my kids of candy and cupcakes, especially at birthdays and special events. It's quite possible to achieve balance if you are mindful—and teach your kids to be mindful—while doing so. Say, "If I eat this now, then later today I should keep sugar out of my body because I want to take care of myself." Hooper also encouraged parents to talk about the fact that food is fuel. It can make you run faster, be stronger, and feel more alert. My kids love talking about those perks because they live for playing sports.

Another way that I try to control sugar intake, at least during the school year, is packing a healthy lunch. If they only have healthy choices, that's what they'll eat.

I've also found that planting a garden can get kids to try new veggies and fruits. Many veggies and fruits we've planted in our garden have been a hit: cantaloupe, pumpkins, sweet peppers, hot peppers, Roma tomatoes, mint, basil, and rosemary. Of course, I am not a green thumb and would never claim to be. For example, one year, a new garden mixed in with some good luck yielded a hugely fantastic watermelon. Asher loved watching it grow and grow . . . and grow some more until the perfect picking day had arrived. He believed he had the watermelon of his dreams. Then we tasted it, and it turned out to be, as Jackson put it, "disgusting." I had chosen a white watermelon plant, which, as it turns out, just doesn't have the same sweet taste of the regular red watermelon we all know and love. Next time, we're just going with the regular watermelon, nothing fancy.

So say you're eating as healthily as you can. What about exercise? A single bout of moderate-to-vigorous physical activity can improve sleep, memory, and the ability to think and learn in addition to reducing anxiety symptoms. Again, let's just make it as plain and simple as possible: kids who don't move are prone to unhealthy lifestyles. So make them move. I understand that if your kid is not "sporty," it makes it more difficult, but pick an activity and just do it. If nothing else, walk. Walk around your neighborhood. Walk to school. Walking is a great way to get the physical activity needed to obtain health benefits without requiring special skills, expensive equipment, or a gym membership.

Think it's not enough? As a parenting journalist, I'd be remiss if I didn't report to you the extraordinary story of eighteen-year-old Michael Watson, a high schooler in Canton, Ohio. Watson had battled with his weight his entire life. But one day during his sophomore year of high school, he decided to make a change. "When I looked in the mirror," Watson said, "I was really ready to get it done and thought, 'I can't just fail anymore on my diet.'"[74] Watson started by walking to and from school every day, more than forty minutes round trip. He walked in the heat and in the rain. Watson also changed his diet, working with his dad to learn how to count calories, then forgoing his normal fast-food meals in exchange for salads, oatmeal, and soup. Eventually, he was featured all over the news for losing 115 pounds, just by changing his diet and walking. Yes, walking.

This is just one example and an extreme one, but it gets right to the point. Educating children about what they are putting into their bodies is powerful. Exercise is powerful, and it doesn't have to be complicated or difficult. Teaching kids to care about themselves, specifically their physical selves, is all part of the journey. We can shape better decisions and healthier choices. It starts with us. So let's all walk the walk and be the inspiration our children need. Think about your circumstances and how you can introduce healthy options into your family's menu while teaching your kids about diet and fitness. It's all about taking a balanced approach. Remember, the topic of this chapter is Acceptance. Kids have to feel loved and beautiful as they are. No one can attain perfection in diet and exercise. (We'll leave attempting it to body builders, or maybe Olympic athletes.)

Pro Parenting Tips: Diet and Nutrition

- Talk about food and nutrition regularly.
- Take a vacation from fast food.
- Cook together. Be a role model in the kitchen. Talk often about preparing a healthy meal.
- Plant a garden.
- Exercise. Get off technology, get outside, and be active any way you can at least once a day. If nothing else, walk.
- Practice mindful eating. Let your child make decisions about what and how much to eat. When you're not around, it's up to her!
- Teach your child to love his body and brain enough to take good care of them.
- Repeat positive affirmations like "As a family, we promote physical health as well as positive mental well-being" and "Our nutrition and exercise are a way of life."

Chapter 3:

Security

If children feel safe, they can take risks, ask questions, make
mistakes, learn to trust, share their feelings, and grow.
—Alfie Kohn

We all need to feel safe and secure to thrive in our world, but a child's
development depends on it. The environment a child lives in determines
whether she feels safe. When we talk about good parenting practices, it
seems obvious that parents should provide their children with physical
safety and security. Physical safety allows the child to know her needs
will be met, that she will be fed, housed, protected, and schooled. But
emotional security is just as crucial. A child needs to know that it's
okay to express her feelings—good, bad, and everything in between.
In addition, she needs the sense of stability that comes from established routines. Parents are supposed to provide their children with the
safest "safe zone" in the world. Providing our children with security is
our superpower and doing so successfully leads to the growth of our
children's own power.

Being Mindful of Our Emotions

Because the emotional security piece of this might not be something
most parents are attuned to, I have made it the focus of this chapter.
As we discuss this vital topic, know that there is no judgment here.
The CASTLE Method is about evolving as parents and looking at how
research on emotions and emotional security can benefit you, your
children, and your family as a whole.

The American Psychological Association defines emotional security as feelings of safety, confidence, and freedom from apprehension.[75] Let's get real: every single one of us can use the practice of expressing and managing our own emotions in moments of frustration and stress. If you learn to better express your emotions, your children will feel more emotionally secure with you. Once that happens, your kids will be better able to share their own feelings and emotions, gaining many positive mental health benefits.

As ever, let's start with what researchers know about the brain and how it handles emotions. Neurologist Dr. Peter Pressman describes it this way: "The brain processes emotions in a series of steps. First, incoming information must be appraised and assigned an emotional value. This process is often very quick and may go beyond our conscious awareness. Even so, our initial emotional reaction depends on several individual biases and contexts. We can then identify and feel the emotion. Depending on the social situation, we may then have to regulate that emotion's expression. For example, there are times where we may want to express rage or disgust but have to keep calm regardless."[76]

When you end up in such situations where controlling your emotions is vital (for example, when your kid is in the middle of a tantrum in public, or he refuses to do his homework), there are simple, healthy steps toward feeling your emotions, managing them, and moving on to more positive emotions. In fact, my award-winning picture book, *Dear Me, Letters to Myself for All of My Emotions*, contains strategies that kids can actually use and practice on their own. Psychologist and Harvard lecturer Rick Weissbourd said of it, "It's vital that children learn to identify and express their feelings and to do so without shame. This engaging, lovely book enables parents to guide their children in doing just that. It gives me hope that more children, rather than running away from feelings, will work to understand them and bring them into their relationships in healthy ways."[77] If you're looking for a simple way to start teaching your children (and yourself) about emotions, *Dear Me* is a great place to start. I sure learned a lot while writing it! In the meantime, try the strategy below, which I've distilled from a variety of sources:

6. Identify the emotion. Ask yourself, "Am I happy, sad, frustrated, scared, etc.?"

7. Allow yourself to *feel* that emotion. No emotion is wrong. It just is.

8. Understand the emotion. Ask yourself, "Why am I frustrated?"

9. Manage the emotion by deep breathing, journaling, and affirming to yourself that the emotion will fade—all science-backed strategies.

10.   Try to move on to a more positive emotion. You are not looking to move immediately from the depths of frustration to the heights of joy, but maybe try going from frustration to a gentle mantra such as "I am okay. I am just fine. I can get through this."

Allowing our emotions to be felt rather than dismissing them provides the emotional security we all need. Children must be able to express their emotions without being quieted by parents, caregivers, coaches, teachers, or any other adults in their world. We must be open to allowing this natural part of life. And when we can model this behavior for our children, their emotional security will run deep and serve them throughout their lives.

By way of example, I'll let you in on a little secret. There are times when I fail to walk the walk on this point, and you can be sure this is what I hear: "Mom, Mom, Mom! You told me to tell you how I feel, to voice my feelings. I'm telling you now. Are you listening to me?"

If you do your best to put those healthy emotional patterns in place, then when you fall short, a reminder from your kid will get you back up to speed, even when you are at your emotional breaking point. In that moment when your baby teaches you, you can say to yourself, "Okay, I am frustrated, but it's okay to be frustrated. I don't like my kid's behavior, but I'll take some deep breaths. This will pass. Let him feel his feelings."

I made sure to say "him" here because I want to add one more note about the emotions of boys in particular. "Boys don't cry" is a stereotype that has persisted for generations. Society expects that boys not express their emotions and often doesn't allow them to.

How Boys Develop Emotionally and Socially

In her book *When Boys Become Boys*, Stanford professor Judy Chu explains that "behaviors typically viewed as 'natural' for boys reflect an adaptation to cultures that require boys to be stoic, competitive, and aggressive if they are to be accepted as 'real boys.' Yet even as boys begin to reap the social benefits of aligning with norms of masculine behavior, they pay a psychological and relational price for renouncing parts of their humanity."[78] They can benefit from this to a degree by gaining acceptance, but the price often includes the ability to empathize, interpret others' emotions, and cultivate meaningful relationships.

Now let's take a closer look at what neuroscientists have found regarding that "nature versus culture" argument. "Studies of infants have shown that neurologically, there isn't much difference between boys' and girls' capacity for empathy. Yet, according to neuroscientists, because girls are allowed to express their emotions, their ability to identify and understand both their own and others' emotions cultivates their empathetic skills beyond those of boys."[79]

To learn what happens after infancy, Dr. Chu studied a group of six boys for two years, beginning when they were four and five years old, the age when boys generally begin to disconnect from their emotions and relationships. When she started, the boys were interpreting emotions well—both their own and others. They also wanted to and knew how to cultivate meaningful relationships. However, midway through kindergarten, they stopped displaying these emotional skills, instead conforming to traditional masculine norms. Dr. Chu concluded that they did this in order to impress and maintain acceptance.[80]

Forbidding our boys to express their emotions not only affects our boys but also our girls, especially later in life when relationships bloom and families are formed. If you have a boy in your family, check your expectations of how he should behave and express his emotions. He, and his future family, will thank you.

Building Parent-Child Relationships

I already mentioned the importance of sharing emotions. Often the result of that sharing is a strong bond with your child, which is equally necessary. In the words of the distinguished developmental psychologist Urie Bronfenbrenner, "in order to develop normally, a child requires progressively more complex joint activity with one or more adults who have an irrational emotional relationship with the child. Somebody's got to be crazy about that kid. That's number one. First, last, and always."[81] Forming a concrete, unconditional, and loving relationship with your child will create a deeper emotional security between the two of you.

I have that "irrational emotional relationship" with my two boys. I bet you do too with your kids. It can sometimes feel illogical, even unreasonable, "irrational," as Bronfenbrenner says. But if you ever feel that you should take a step back and put the brakes on your inner mama bear (or papa bear), hold on. When you see what the research indicates, you'll know that you can trust your intuition, that it's leading you along the right path. You are giving your child what she needs most: your unconditional love.

An Environment of Relationships

The Harvard Center for the Developing Child has said, "Nurturing and stable relationships with caring adults are essential to healthy human development beginning from birth. Early, secure attachments contribute to the growth of a broad range of competencies, including a love of learning, a comfortable sense of oneself, positive social skills, multiple successful relationships at later ages, and a sophisticated understanding of emotions, commitment, morality, and other aspects of human relationships. Stated simply, establishing successful relationships with adults and other children provides a foundation of capacities that children will use for a lifetime."[82]

It's easy to get into the trap of being busy, but show a true interest in your child. The reality is that you only have a short period of time with your children. Research shows that if a child has at least one parent or caregiver who is present—who shows up—she can thrive. Longitudinal research on child development suggests that one of the best predictors for how any child turns out—in terms of happiness, social and emotional development, meaningful relationships, and even academic and career success—is having received sensitive, supportive care early in life.[83]

Pro Parenting Tips: Showing Interest

- Be present for your child—physically and emotionally. Take a break from tech and be present in everyday conversations.
- Be interested in his interests and passions. Ask him about his dreams, big and small.
- Find ways to connect that are meaningful to your child. Make special time for you to share, one on one, without other family members.
- Have open lines of communication, always.
- When mistakes are made, be gentle and let your child know you love him no matter what.

Making a Family Mission Statement

Another way to provide an emotionally secure space for your kids is to establish routines, which grant children stability and a sense of belonging to something greater than themselves.

That sense of belonging is imperative. According to Jennifer Wickham, a licensed professional counselor in behavioral health, "having a sense of belonging is so important, considering the groups and labels we give ourselves and others. We are members of families, sporting teams, hobbyists, spiritual groups, charities, political parties, cities, countries, and nationalities, to name a few. Nearly every aspect of our lives is organized around belonging to something."[84] A sense of belonging is the way that humankind organizes itself. If belonging wasn't important, we would live solitary lives. We wouldn't have families or organized communities or government. Belonging is a protective factor. It tells us we have support from the ones we hold close, and it plays into our physical and mental health. When children feel as though they belong unconditionally to a family unit, they can feel safe no matter what the world throws at them.

But feeling as though you belong to a family doesn't just happen on its own; it requires intentionality. It also requires that organization that Wickham describes. So how might parents go about organizing a family? A good jumping-off point is to craft a family mission statement.

A mission statement is a summary of what matters most to you as a family. Your mission statement can be an outline of the foundation for all family interactions, activities, and structure. The key word here is "summary"; your statement does not need to be long.

When creating a mission statement, make sure you do it together as a family. If you as parents involve your kids in setting clear guidelines, the communication that follows will, per the Child Development Institute, "engender a sense of belonging to the group, as all the members work toward the same goals."[85] Kids will feel a sense of belonging as their voices are heard, their ideas are accepted, and thoughtful reflection becomes the norm.

The mission statement also gives everyone a clear understanding of what is expected of them and how the family will work together. One study found that while seven out of ten parents say they have an explicit set of values for their family, only three out of ten have those values in writing, as a mission statement or otherwise.[86] Corporations, schools, and other large organizations rely on mission statements to keep their communities together, to understand expectations, and to achieve the goals the organization is founded on. Don't you think your most important "community" deserves just as much thought and effort?

Research tells us that our family is currently the institution that most defines us. Family is ranked by American adults as more central to their identity than any other surveyed factor (i.e., nationality, faith, ethnicity, etc.). But this statistic is changing with the new generation. Only slightly more than half of all "Millennials" (53%) say that family plays a significant role ("a lot"), compared to over three-quarters of "Elders" (76%).[87] Despite these shifts, you as parents can still take building your child's character seriously. Discuss virtues like self-control, patience, fairness, and conflict resolution with your child on a daily basis. When it comes to preserving your family, it's comforting to know you're all on the same page, both parents and kids. Making a mission statement will give you that knowledge, creating that sense of belonging and security in this, the most important community in your—and your children's—lives.

There is no wrong way to create a family mission statement. It doesn't have to be a serious document. Try to embody the spirit of your family and have fun with it. One way I like to do it is by using affirmative statements, such as: "We believe in . . ." "We strive for . . ." "We are . . ." etc. The Mindful Little Minds website has a great summary of how to go about creating a family mission statement.[88] For now, here are some easy steps to get you started:

First, as parents, discuss what is important to you. Ask yourself and your partner, "What do we value in the growth and development of our family? What matters to us as parents? What matters to our kids? What do we expect our family to be?" When you start thinking about what your family mission statement will provide, it may seem relatively easy, but to set the foundation for a great family and sustain the values and commitments expressed in the statement, it's a good idea to really think this through. We want our families to be secure in their sense of belonging and in our family system and values. And be open to allowing new values to evolve. Each family's mission statement will look and feel different based on culture, religious ideals, and unique family dynamics.

Next, call a family meeting and share your ideas and thoughts with your children. Ask your children to share their ideas and thoughts. (This is all dependent on age, but each member should have a voice.) As leaders of the family, you can, if you wish, easily incorporate the fundamental building blocks outlined in the CASTLE Method: "We are a compassionate family, we are an accepting family, we value security for all in the family, we believe trust is essential in our family, we love our family, we have certain expectations of our family, and we value education in this family."

Here are some questions to consider in your discussion:

- What is important to us as a family?
- What do we believe in as a family?
- How do we want it to feel in our family?
- What do we enjoy doing together as a family?
- How do we treat people as a family?
- What do we want to do more of as a family?
- How do we show our love and respect for each other in our family?

Ask an older child to write out the statement. Little ones can assist. This is where you can get more concrete and move into more specifics that match your unique family. Here's more of what's on my family's list:

- kindness and empathy
- leadership
- respect
- spiritual and religious values
- family work ethic
- family time
- family traditions
- financial values
- family health and fitness
- family tech time
- inspiration and creativity
- antiracist (a recent addition)

Have fun and enjoy the process of creating your family mission statement. Throughout the meeting, the entire family should discuss each part of the mission statement so that everyone understands. Once the document is complete, decorate it as a family, and hang it up somewhere in the house (such as the laundry room or kitchen) where all can see but only family members can access. As you all evolve as individuals and family members, you can adjust and re-create your statement, but now you will have the foundation for who your family is, what you seek to achieve, and how you will live in your family community and the rest of the world.

Pro Parenting Tips: Family Mission Statements

- Brainstorm as a family.
- Ask your kids to be the experts.
- Walk the walk.
- Be open to new values: As the world evolves, remember that we must be open to change.
- Practice compassion as you live out your family values.
- Love and cherish your family values.
- Expect that you and your children will live your values every day to the best of your ability. Be understanding of mistakes and miscommunications.

Tackling Technology Appropriately

Any parent reading this book has had to deal with technology and how kids use it. And I am the first one to say that I have not always loved technology for kids. It has grown on me as I've learned to understand it better and see some of the benefits. But it has been a journey. Here's a little taste of how it started in our home.

When Jackson was six and Asher was five, they were allowed fifteen "iPad minutes" (what we called screen time) each day. That didn't include TV time, which was separately limited. But as summer set in, my boys seemed to want screen time more and more—and more. Soon Asher was yelling and screaming that his time was not up (when it was) and holding onto the iPad with a serious death grip. I'd literally have to pry it out of his hands. It was creeping into our lives in a very ugly way, and I'd had enough!

This decision was a bit scary for me. I knew it would undoubtedly cause me more trouble than I could handle. However, we (my husband and I) thought it was what was best for our family at the time. I wouldn't allow my children to be addicted to useless games and hours of meaningless activity. While I love technology and believe it has some benefits for children, I do not think it serves young children well, educational games included. Just because it's there doesn't mean it's necessary or even okay. I just see hours of technology use as a bad habit. And for my kids at least, it's a privilege, not a right. So, here's how the summer 2014 "no technology experiment" went down in our household, with all the detours we enjoyed—yes, I meant to write "enjoyed."

To soften the blow, we gave the boys the news while they were busy drawing superheroes: They were cut off. No iPad, no internet, no older cousins' iPhones, no nothing, all summer long. But it didn't seem to set in because they didn't really seem to care. All they said was "Okay." *What?* Did they not understand what we just said? I wondered when it was going to sink in.

In the first week, the boys probably asked to use the iPad about five times. Each time I stated firmly, "No, not until the end of the summer," but inside I was afraid of the tantrum to follow. Amazingly, there was only a bit of whining and asking when summer would end. (A strange question from kids, but I guess in this context it does make sense.) Still, that was it. *Really.*

In July, the boys were busy with kindergarten and first-grade camp and zoo camp and theater camp. We took a trip to San Diego, which filled a few of their days. Swimming was also a biweekly activity. At home, the backyard served them well; they played soccer and putted around on the putting green. Jackson's first book club meeting had us busy reading *Charlie and the Chocolate Factory*, and more reading followed. The point is that they didn't really miss technology. It kind of felt like the summers I had enjoyed as a kid, with lots of downtime, lots of playtime, and lots of fun.

At the start of August, the boys spent time with family—both casual visits and nights of never-ending cousin sleepovers. I would occasionally ask the boys—no, really tell them—okay, work *extraordinarily hard* to brainwash them about the effects of too much technology and screen time on their developing brains. At times they really bought into it, declaring, "Mommy, even when we can use the iPad again, we won't," followed by "It's just bad for your brain." *Yeeeesssssssss!* My plan was working!

The first detour came in mid-August: a friend's birthday party. This party was not to be missed for two reasons. One, my boys love this kid— so do I—and two, there was the well-known fact that a video-game truck would be part of the festivities. That second one presented the first serious challenge to our technology fast. What to do? For me, it was simple. This was a way to show the boys that video games and technology can be all right, just as long as they're used wisely. Not to mention this was a special occasion. So the boys attended the party, which also included gobs of sugar displays (first a cake, then an ice cream truck, and for the grand finale, a piñata). It was fun, and sometimes you've just got to let loose. The boys played the games, but I didn't have to pry them out of the truck. (The sugar helped do that!)

We were now headed into the final week before school started, and the sun had set on summer. The no-technology experiment was just about complete—and then came the mammoth-sized detour we were so fatefully guaranteed. We came upon it during our family's last hurrah of the season, a trip to Amelia Island in Florida. The boys took the flight in stride. In place of headphones or the iPad, they slept, ate, talked, and played their own made-up mind-reading game with sticks (very old-school). We were a bit loud, but I don't think we bothered too many people. On to the hotel. There, out of nowhere, we found a shock for us all that none of us could have ever imagined: the most un-believable, magnificent, flashing game room ever. The magical noises inside the room drew kids in like zombies, ready for them to jump onto black leather gaming seats, grab onto a huge assortment of hand-held devices, and become mesmerized by screens for hours—possibly days. The teenager running the room even said, "If there's a game you'd like to play, and we don't have it, we'll get it for you." I'm not kidding! Forget *Charlie and the Chocolate Factory*. This was *Charlie and the Video Game Factory*.

This did not look good. We had been practically technology-free all summer long. We were only a week away from success. How could I keep them away from this game room, which we would pass by at least half a dozen times a day, every single day, for five days? You may be surprised to hear that, again, it was simple. We were on vacation, and my boys might never again see this amazing world that only a kid could truly appreciate (except perhaps for some dads I know). So we let them in and let them have at it. To be fair, we did tell them this was one of those special occasions.

After that, all was well in their world and ours. We filled their days with swimming at the pool, swimming in the ocean, searching for shark teeth (Jackson found sixteen, Asher, none—that was not fun), collecting and examining seashells, and lots more. Then at night, the boys, along with their cousins, were allowed to go to the game room— on their own, I might add—and just play *video games*.

It was done. GAME OVER. We had fallen a week short in our exper-iment. Still, it was okay.

How have we moved forward since then? Before the 2014 summer ban on technology, the boys were allowed fifteen minutes a day on the iPad. They were five and six years old then. At the time of writing, they are eleven and twelve. Now, the technology rule is no iPad or technology during the school week, unless it's for school. They get minimal TV time, which they mostly use to watch sports and cartoons. On the weekends, they can have extended tech time. And it works quite well for us.

As you work to find the right balance in your home—your castle—just know this is an ongoing process. Not too long ago, I had to re-introduce some tech expectations when the boys got into fantasy football. They are on their phones a lot, looking up players and statistics and texting with friends about trades. And my way is not the only way. You have to decide what will work for you and your children. If you are aware of what your kids are doing with technology and engaging with them in their technology use, you can find that balance. There's lots of learning and lots of friendship building going on when my boys use tech for fantasy football. Heck, I see that as a positive.

So what principles should you build your technology guidelines on? One bit of wisdom that really resonates for me is from one of my interviewees on the technology topic. Dr. Leonard Sax, author of the New York Times best seller *The Collapse of Parenting: How We Hurt Our Kids When We Treat Them Like Adults* gave me a clear perspective.

During our interview, he asked me, "Did your parents allow you to take phone calls from a boy, or a girl for that matter, at eleven p.m. or midnight when you were a kid?"

"Of course not!" I stated. There was no way my mom would allow that.

"Exactly." He followed that up with this: "So why in the world are kids, tweens, and teens taking their cell phones into bed at night and texting and talking and who knows what?"

Yep, I get it. While trust is one of the building blocks of the CASTLE Method (see chapter 4), and it's important to trust your children to make some decisions for themselves, parents still need to set limits.

Period. We don't have enough research yet to say for sure what effect technology has on children's developing brains, and until we do, we need to exercise caution. In Dr. Robin Berman's book *Permission to Parent: How to Raise Your Child with Love and Limits*, she gives this advice: "Regulate media so it doesn't steal childhood. Monitor and have rules for young kids; teach older ones to monitor themselves. And electronics, games, and videos are addictive. Teach moderation."[89] I liken it to the limits we set on drinking until children are of age. You wouldn't say, "Sure, have a drink," to your sixteen-year-old, and you wouldn't leave the choice of when to start drinking up to her either.

My boys are on the cusp of those teenage years, and I know that helping them live a healthy tech life is just another part of parenting in this generation. Take it from me as a teacher: children can accept and even appreciate limits, and as long as we set proper expectations, technology doesn't have to be the enemy. And if your child says he's bored and that there's nothing else to do, take a deep breath, acknowledge what he's feeling, and then stand your ground. It's absolutely possible to maintain a healthy relationship with your child and keep the rules you've set at the same time.

Fast Forward to the "Fortnite Explosion"

As I've already stated, you have to find a way to make technology work in your home. That is an ongoing process, with many pros and cons to consider. Video games in and of themselves are not bad. When we see them as our kids' version of entertainment, we can look at them in the ways that we might classify movies or TV. Ask yourself questions like "Is this game age appropriate? Do I feel comfortable with this type of violence (if any)? Is this game becoming addictive and/or distracting my child from everyday life?"

Now, as a teaching tool for you, I'll share a story, and you can decide what you'd do in this situation.

Fortnite is an online multiplayer game that allows people all over the planet to battle it out in different settings, using weapons such as machine guns and swords. There are two modes: Players battle each other in Fortnite Battle Royale for the chance to be the last one standing. In Fortnite Save the World, players collaborate to fight off waves of encroaching monsters. At time of writing, 150 million people are obsessed with *Fortnite*. And that obsession is creating a battle of its own in homes from coast to coast: kids versus parents and even parents versus parents.

It was nearly noon Pacific Standard Time on a Tuesday in 2018, and *Fortnite* fanatics all around the world were waiting for the revelation about the fate of the "Tilted Towers." In sunny Southern California, kids at a Los Angeles school (which will remain unnamed to protect all involved) were just getting out of their fifth-grade science class. According to the teacher who told me this story, "the kids lined up at the door and rushed out of class. Eighteen boys ran across the field, almost knocking down one teacher" as they headed to the first computer they could find.[90] Their mission? To Google what had happened in the Fortnite saga.

Administrators were shocked to hear that the boys were bypassing the school's rules and regulations just to satisfy their need to know. It looked like extreme addictive behavior. That led to what this teacher calls an important digital citizenship moment. "We had a conversation with the kids to help them understand that Fortnite cannot impact school time. Parents also received an email to continue the discussion at home."

The email was welcome, as parents everywhere expressed their anxiety about the game. The usual homework debate was replaced by the Fortnite debate. It's all parents were talking about when they were getting together. It permeated every community in the country and was becoming a major concern for many parents as they wrestled with the violent and addictive nature of the game.

What would you do in their place? Here is what some experts and parents have to say on the topic.

Dr. Dean Leav is a clinical psychologist who works with video game addicts. I have interviewed Dr. Leave many times over the years for his expertise and insights. Regarding *Fortnite*, he says that it does involve collaboration and competition, which makes it appealing to kids of all different ages.[91] Sometimes, it can be too appealing.

In the Eleventh International Classification of Diseases, the World Health Organization includes "gaming disorder" in its list of mental health conditions.[92] Dr. Leav says, "That's a huge first step. The world is seeing more and more the impact of gaming addiction on children." In one study, phone interviews with nearly three thousand American college students between 2007 and 2015 revealed that roughly one in twenty experienced "disturbances in daily life" as a result of their internet gaming habits, which Dr. Maurice Ohayon says is a requirement for an addiction to be considered a disorder.[93] And when young people get addicted, "it may trigger sleep difficulties, depression, anxiety and, in some cases, even suicidal thoughts."[94]

Over the years, I've also interviewed parents like you to get a sense of how they approach the question of video game limits. In Los Angeles, one mom's ten-year-old son was feeling left out because she didn't allow him to play *Fortnite*. He told her, "I don't really want to go to school because PE, lunch, and recess are so boring because all anyone does is talk about *Fortnite*." But this mom remained strong: "We should be teaching our kids not to glamorize violence, especially in the era of school shootings."[95]

Another L.A. mom says *Fortnite* has a hold on her ten-year-old son unlike any other video game before. In fact, she's had to adjust her son's "tech contract" (i.e. his tech privileges) because, during a recent playdate, her son played *Fortnite* alone in his room instead of playing ping pong with his guests. "His contract has a clause that if friends are over, [he] need[s] to get permission to play *Fortnite*. If granted, it will be for a limited time, and only if everyone wants to play and has their own device to play on. At no point may you play *Fortnite* without your friend(s)."[96]

Boston mom Gail Miller says *Fortnite* was consuming her household. Miller has two sons, ages eleven and seven. For her eleven-year-old, playing the video game is about socializing. "He's on the shy side, so this is a real bonding experience for him. They play online together and try to work together. If I didn't let him play, he would feel really left out."[97] However, her seven-year-old is not allowed to play, and Gail is aware of other parents who don't want any of their kids to play. She respects that.

In Houston, Dani Roisman's nine-year-old son was caught up in *Fortnite* just like all of his friends—that is, until Dani took a closer look. In Roisman's opinion, tactical shooting and weaponry is not what kids should be thinking about. "We broke the bad news to our son that he could no longer play it, and we explained to him that we don't think it's age appropriate."[98]

Roisman's judgment is supported by Common Sense Media, a non-profit organization whose website provides age-based media reviews for families.[99] They suggest *Fortnite* is for thirteen years and up. Sierra Filucci, executive editor of parenting content and distribution for Common Sense Media, explains that their "guides are not hard and fast rules and that they are based on child-development guidelines that take a lot of different issues into consideration."[100]

Why thirteen and up? Filucci says there are three factors: "First, the violence. Although the visual is cartoonish, the main objective is to kill. Second, consumerism. The pressure to buy battle passes or skins—that kind of marketing toward kids is not necessarily a good thing. And third, the open chats. Depending on the mode, your child could have a conversation with anyone (a stranger) that the game matches them to."

Dr. Leav recommends that, if kids are playing *Fortnite*, to play with them. It's also important to engage in conversations with younger kids about what's real and not real. "Real people don't respond after getting shot. Real people don't heal immediately after being stabbed, and these things are happening in Fortnite. There's no medic in real life, on site, who will instantly save you."

And if your kid is playing *Fortnite*, or any other video game for that matter, limits are vital. "Thirty minutes or less a day during the school week," Dr. Leav recommends, "whether a kid is under thirteen or over thirteen. Kids have so many obligations. They have to do their homework, chores, and after-school activities. If they're spending two to three hours per day [on video games], life is not balanced."

What about summertime? No more than one or two hours a day is Dr. Leav's advice. "After the one- or two-hour mark, you can see that the child is being affected by the video games. You can see that they are spacing out, that they are not engaging as much with other people, that their body and posture are changing. That's the time to unplug."

Fortnite doesn't seem to be going away anytime soon, and the next video-game craze is likely nearing beta, "approaching launch in the very near future!" (Remember *Pokémon Go*?) But kids and parents don't have to be caught up in the chaos. At that Los Angeles school, kids now know the *Fortnite* distraction is unacceptable during school hours. Teachers have started challenging kids to break the mold and focus their attention on other types of entertainment. Believe it or not, the next new fad for the fifth-grade boys was the Rubik's Cube. Teachers say it's a step in the right direction. "At lunch and recess, the Rubik's Cube is the preferred game of choice for some boys, replacing the *Fortnite* talk" and bringing kids back into the real world.

Pro Parenting Tips: How to Set Boundaries around Tech Time

- State the rules and adaptations to the rules clearly. Write out a technology contract or add a tech section to your family mission statement. This is a great way to ensure that everyone is on the same page.
- Be firm but be flexible too. If you restrict screen time, replace it with a new activity.

- Teach kids that consumer skepticism is good, that they shouldn't immediately jump at any shiny new tech toy or game. This teaches tech literacy.
- Be realistic with expectations. Understand that your kids are digital natives, and that technology is a part of their lives.
- As kids grow, teach them how to manage their own screen time.
- Really know what you and your child are getting into before you dive into any kind of social media apps.
- Learn how to protect your child in the cyber world. Use internet screening services to block inappropriate content when your kids are browsing. It's a part of modern parenting. (And no surprise, that's what the next section is all about.)

Parents, You're Not Done Yet: Technology and Pornography

I wish I didn't even have to address this topic. But the reality is that I have to. To do so, I rely on one of the most well-versed experts in the field today. Dr. Gail Dines has researched and written about the porn industry for more than thirty years and is internationally acclaimed as the leading expert on how pornography shapes our identities, culture, and sexuality. She is the founder of Culture Reframed and a consultant to government agencies in the United States and abroad. I first saw her speak at an LA public elementary school, where parents walked away wanting to protect their kids, only years away from being teens, from this catastrophic awareness of what Dr. Dines calls "the public health crisis of the digital age."[101]

Dr. Dines's research shows that early access to pornography

undermines the healthy social, sexual, emotional, and cognitive development of young people and that it's only a click away. In short, it's free, it's violent, and it's based on the abuse and degradation of women and people of color. When I heard her speak, I decided I needed to know more and interviewed her for my podcast. Here are the facts from her about kids and porn:

- Thirty-nine percent of fourteen-year-olds report having seen porn, with about one-third of young people saying they had seen it for the first time at age twelve or younger.
- Minors who view pornography and other sexualized media are more accepting of sexual violence.
- Boys who increase their use of online porn show a decrease in academic performance in as soon as six months.
- Fifteen years old is the average age at which teens first receive a sext.
- A significant relationship exists for teens between frequent pornography use and feelings of loneliness and major depression.
- A study of fourteen- to nineteen-year-olds found that young women who consumed pornographic videos were at a significantly greater risk of being victims of sexual harassment or sexual assault.
- Teens who view pornography are disoriented during the developmental phase, the time when they must learn how to handle their sexuality and are most vulnerable to uncertainty about their sexual beliefs and moral values.

Children who are exposed to porn are at higher risk to develop unhealthy habits as they grow into adulthood. They are often confused about what a good sexual relationship looks like and feels like. And sadly, when kids grow into adults, they bring that porn and those distorted values into their new families. Doing so has a variety of negative effects, including the following:

- Forty-seven percent of families in the United States reported that pornography is a problem in their home.
- Pornography use increases the marital infidelity rate by more than 300 percent.

- Forty percent of people identified as "sex addicts" lose their spouses, 58 percent suffer considerable financial losses, and about 33 percent lose their jobs.
- Forty-four percent of divorce cases involve one party meeting a new paramour over the internet, while 56 percent involve one party having an "obsessive interest" in the pornographic.[102]

On the *Dr. Phil Show*, Dr. Phil has been exposing what our children are up against on the internet for years. Pornography sites and their availability to our children are exploding. With all his experience, he summed his stance up in a one-on-one interview in 2019 when he told me, "Invade your kids' privacy!"[103]

He added, "Kids have the knowledge but not the wisdom to use the internet. We have the wisdom but not the knowledge. That's got to merge in some way. Parents need to get on the platforms their kids are on. Sometimes parents will say that they're invading their kid's privacy. I say, 'Invade it.' You need to know where your kids are. People won't take a position. I am taking a position. Invade your kid's privacy, know where they are, know who they're talking to. The internet is just bringing all kinds of information into the home. There's just a lot of distraction, a lot of competition for the parent's voice to resonate in the children's ears. So, you need to make sure that you're the best voice in your children's ears."

So Dr. Phil and Dr. Dines agree that we must educate parents and kids about the dangers of the internet, and they advise parents to get involved and set limits. If we let porn into our homes now, we will be allowing it to shape future generations. The negative effects of pornography do not end after childhood. They can be just as harmful to your kids' future families and marriages. Educate your kids to protect their physical and mental health. Go to CultureReframed.org. This program, founded by Dr. Dines herself, is one of the best resources for understanding not only how to educate yourself, but also how to talk to your kids and teens—in an age-appropriate way. Dr. Dines even has scripts for you to follow. You can do this! You are protecting your children and their future kids.

I hope that this chapter has given you a new way to think about security in your castle. Providing security for our children, both physical and emotional, is a significant building block, and there are a lot of aspects to consider, but please believe that it's possible. Just take it day by day, one step at a time, and I promise you and your kids will get to where you want to be.

Chapter 4:

Trust

Never help a child with
a task at which he feels he can succeed.
—Maria Montessori

As leaders in our castles, we as parents must give our children guidance and support. We must make the big decisions our children cannot be expected to make. We have to help them get to school in the morning, make their doctor's appointments and then get them there—all the things adults have to do that children cannot . . . yet.

But what about what they *can* do now? When you think about truly trusting your children to make decisions about their needs, regardless of yours, you may feel some anxiety. What if they choose wrong? But by trusting your children anyway, you are allowing them to grow and develop and, most importantly, learn to trust themselves. For this internal growth to happen, we must step aside and allow it.

Here's an example. When your child can tie her own shoes, but it just takes a very long time, let her. Even better, build that time and space into your morning routine so that there's no pressure on you to tie her shoes for her and rush her out the door to school. Of course, not every morning will allow for this practice, but every time you can manage, it will teach your child that you trust her to do what she can, providing a building block of trust that will spill into the rest of your child's life. By planting this trust early in life, you will be setting your child up to have confidence in her ability, her decision making, and her inherent knowledge of what's best for her. Isn't that what you want for your children when they someday leave your castle for their own independent journey in life?

Imagine the opposite future for a minute. If you don't allow this fundamental growth, your child may decide he can't trust his own judgment. As he grows into a teenager and then an adult, as he looks toward his peers and away from you, he may end up trusting someone untrustworthy, with dangerous consequences. Children must learn to eventually follow their own best judgment, and you as a parent can provide a safe space for them to do that.

Now, like so many things in parenting, learning to trust your children is a work in progress. In my home, I must remind myself over and over again: *Just trust.* As a starting point, here's a quote by Lady Bird Johnson that really resonates with me: "Encourage and support your kids because children are apt to live up to what you believe of them." So whenever I finish having a discussion with my boys—about school, friends, or extracurriculars—I say, "Okay, I trust you. I trust that you know what is best for you." I believe saying these words out loud to them gives them the boost they need, telling them that they can make good decisions and do what they can in this moment in time. I do trust my kids, and I want them to understand they've got the green light from me to trust themselves.

Let Them Lead: The Power of "No"

The weekend was winding down, and the four of us had headed out for a Sunday matinee. We had decided to watch the PG-rated film *Miracles from Heaven*, a story about a ten-year-old girl who has a rare, incurable disease. The mother becomes a fierce advocate for her daughter, and the film eventually ends with the young girl recovering from her illness in what can only be described as a miracle.

But we never got to see the miracle. About a third of the way through the movie, eight-year-old Jackson tugged on my arm and said, "I want to leave."

"Why? What's wrong?" I whispered back.

"I just can't watch this. I want to go now."

I didn't understand. He got up and walked out. I followed, while my husband, Andrew, and Asher remained in the theater.

Sitting with him outside, I did everything in my power to talk Jackson into going back in. He wouldn't budge. After a few minutes, I told him I would wait with him until the end of the movie. Just then, Andrew came out, Asher in tow, and started trying to convince Jackson to come back in. Jackson was adamant he wouldn't go back, saying it was "too scary."

Finally, we decided to leave. My husband, being the frugal one, went to explain our predicament to the ticket takers and get a refund. As we headed toward our car, Andrew and Asher started talking about sports, but Jackson was quiet. I was too, but I took his hand and smiled at him.

Then, just as we were about to get into the car, Jackson said to me, "Mommy, thank you. I feel respected."

Wow, I thought to myself. *What a lesson!*

At that moment I knew I needed to practice trusting him more often. I had to allow my kids to say no to me when they needed to, even if it was uncomfortable or inconvenient for me. I knew this would teach them more than I could imagine.

According to professionals, the power of saying no is a gift. Dr. Ramani Durvasula told me, "Saying no allows children to learn to advocate for themselves. It can keep them safe. They learn to say no to peer pressure around drugs, sex, or other potentially risky behavior, to develop their sense of self, and to learn to appropriately voice a preference."[104] Parents also need to teach their kids when and where it's appropriate to voice that preference: "Saying no to the history test probably won't work. . . . This isn't about entitlement or acting out, but rather about self-advocacy."

This concept of self-advocacy is in practice every day at UCLA Lab

School, where teaching strategies are focused on helping students truly trust themselves. This on-campus laboratory school currently serves students ranging in age from four through twelve and has a re-search-based "Safe School" philosophy that is all about empowering children by teaching them to be problem solvers and inclusive self-ad-vocates. Laurie A. Nimmo-Ramirez, the Safe School Demonstration Teacher, says they begin this work with children at age four, through role play and classroom projects, and continue as students get older.

> We work to keep the language around telling someone "Stop" or "No" current and age appropriate. As students mature, we are more thoughtful about how to address issues around peer pressure and exiting a situation. We also know that as students get older, they are not as willing to come to an adult for help. We need to give them the tools to say no independently and with confidence. . . . Ava de La Sota, who led our school in the development of our Safe School approach and my predecessor, used to always say, "If they can't exit cool, they won't exit." We want to provide our students opportunities to practice these strategies using realistic scenarios (as realistic as a simulation can be) with the hope they will apply them in their lives.[105]

In addition to teaching these strategies in the classroom, UCLA Lab School also uses actual conflicts that occur between the students every day as learning opportunities to practice and discuss the strategies they have been taught. Nimmo-Ramirez says, "We identify the strat-egies they used (or didn't use) and how the choices they made either helped or escalated the problem. We work to unpack the situation so we can talk about how things could be handled differently by making different choices next time. Many times, these conversations (we call them mediations) include discussions about standing up for yourself, saying, 'Stop it,' and when necessary, exiting a situation."

This topic found its way into our conversation one evening when

I was having dinner with a friend of mine. Carol is a stay-at-home mother of two young kids. She describes her six-year-old son Teddy as "not very sporty." Rather, he's that kid who creates and builds. Give him some Legos and it's amazing what he can come up with. All his friends, though, are very sporty, playing in every league imaginable. Carol told me that when soccer season was on the horizon, the "sporty boy" moms would exchange long email threads on the topic, and she felt pressured to sign Teddy up. Even though she was unsure about moving forward, she ultimately did to keep Teddy from feeling left out—or so she thought.

When she told Teddy he was on the soccer roster, "he was very adamant that he didn't want to play, but I ignored him. When we went to buy all the gear, he cried, but I ignored him. When we got to the first practice, he was very clingy and had no interest, but I pushed him. I finally realized after three practices that I was doing this for me, not him. When we got home, I sat him down and asked him if he wanted to do this. He answered with a resounding 'No!' He explained to me why he felt this way. I finally heard him."

Carol had realized her son deserved his own voice. She said she wants to raise her two children to feel empowered by their own decisions, and she believes she must start cultivating that power now.

According to Dr. Durvasula, now is indeed the time. As a clinical psychologist, she sees adults struggle to say no a lot in their everyday lives: "People are often afraid of disappointing other people, especially in the workplace, and can exhaust themselves in the process of saying yes to demanding partners, demanding co-workers, demanding family, and demanding friends. Life is about choices, and when we learn to say no at a younger age, we may be in a better position to execute the 'Power of No' in a more consistent way as adults." Women are especially susceptible to this.

I admit I am one of those adults who struggles with saying no. But now I remember the possible benefits for my children, and every time

I am reminded that I am their role model. If they see me say no when it's appropriate, I hope they will follow my example and learn how to say no with conviction and confidence as they grow and experience the world on their own.

Pro Parenting Tips: Encourage Trust in You and in Themselves

- Teach your child to be a self-advocate. Ask him how he's feeling and reward him for volunteering his thoughts in appropriate situations.
- When your child is showing distress, be compassionate. Listen intently when she tells you how she feels and let her know you trust her to know her own feelings.
- Teach your child that you trust him. Let him be a problem solver by allowing him to act alone or with minimal support in age-appropriate tasks.

Quitting versus Changing Course: Extracurricular Activities

With Carol's experience in mind, I'd like to begin this section with a question for you. As a reporter, I love asking questions. In fact, let's imagine I have a TV crew with me and that you and I are sitting on a couch preparing for an interview. Maybe this is an "off the record" interview, so we can even have cocktails.

Okay. Here's the question: When you were five years old, or eight, or nine, or even twelve or thirteen, did you know what you'd be doing for the rest of your life?

Now take a moment and think back to that kid *you* were. Did you really, *really* know? I certainly didn't. When I was a kid, I enjoyed so many different activities. As a student at St. Stephen's Elementary

School, I played every sport I could find: volleyball, basketball, track, and more. I enjoyed school, and I was on the student council in both seventh and eighth grades. I even played the piano. Not once did I feel pressure of any kind—from my parents, that is. But one day in eighth grade, a brief and stern conversation took place with my piano teacher that changed the course of what made me *me*.

It was 5:15 at night, and I was fifteen minutes late for my piano lesson. My mother dropped me off at the lesson and left to get one of my brothers to another activity.

I sat down at the piano, and my teacher sat next to me. She was furious.

She said, "You know you are late?"

"Yes. I'm sorry."

"You have your concert this week," she said. "How can you be late when you have to prepare for your concert?"

I tried to explain that I had been at basketball practice, and I had tried my best to get out on time, but our team meeting had gone a little long. We were preparing for the championship game, and I was the team captain.

She wouldn't accept it. She had no empathy. She told me it was unacceptable. I felt horrible. I hated to disappoint anyone. Then she said something I will never forget.

"Donna," she said, "you have to choose: piano or basketball."

I was in shock. I couldn't believe what I was hearing. I didn't answer.

After that, we went on with the lesson. It was miserable. All I could think about was having to make that choice. I was only twelve.

When the lesson finally ended, I started to get up from the piano. Again, she said, "You have to choose: piano or basketball."

I was really upset at that point and said, "I choose basketball." Then I thanked her and went outside to wait for my mom.

I performed at my concert that weekend and enjoyed it, but I never took another piano lesson.

As a mom, I now look back at that experience and feel ripped off. I know now that I was never going to be a pro basketball player nor a professional pianist. But why in the world did I have to give up music? I didn't love practicing an hour a day, but I loved playing and had played for many years. I also loved basketball. Why couldn't I have done both? Why did this teacher interfere with my passions? Why did she make me feel as if it was one or the other? In fact, why couldn't I have taken a break from piano for a few weeks or months to finish my basketball season and then dive back into piano? Why so much pressure? Why such finality?

I tell this story because our kids are facing pressure unlike ever before to make decisions about a future they can barely imagine. Did you know that, according to a poll from the National Alliance for Youth Sports, 70 percent of kids have played and then quit an organized sport by age thirteen?[106] According to the Music Parents' Guide, "every year almost 100% of public-school students begin an instrument through their school's music program (if a program exists). One or two years later, more than 50% of students quit, unable to enjoy all that music education has to offer for the rest of their K–12 schooling, if not beyond."[107] Why is quitting a trend?

Here's a possible contributing factor: Culturally, we are teaching our kids that if they aren't competitive in a sport or any other extracurricular activity, it is not worthwhile. We are taking the fun out of learning and playing. For me, that mentality not only rings true but sounds off like a fire alarm. Here are just some of the statements I've heard from the "man on the street" (MOSs in TV lingo) when I asked parents about extracurricular activities:

- Parents of a preschooler: "We need to hire a consultant to make sure our daughter gets into the best kindergarten in LA, because she is going to be a dancer, and we need a school with the best theater department."
- Mom of a fourth-grade son who plays soccer: "I've gotta find a club

soccer program and get him going to see if he's really gonna play soccer in college."

- Mom of a sixth-grade son who plays baseball: "We're not going to go to a demanding school for seventh grade because we need to dedicate all our time to practice baseball."

- Parents of an eleventh-grade daughter preparing for college: "If she doesn't get into her number one Ivy League school, she is going to be devastated. She has done every extracurricular activity you can think of."

These MOSs' words may be difficult to swallow, but that's the reality for a lot of kids.

Here are some eye-opening real-life sports statistics. Many children grow up dreaming of playing sports in college and beyond, but of the nearly 8 million students currently participating in high school athletics in the United States, only 495,000 of them will ever compete at NCAA schools, and only a fraction will realize their goal of becoming a professional or Olympic athlete.[108] As an example, here's the NCAA data on baseball from 2016: Out of 1,206 MLB draft picks, only 695 of them were from NCAA schools. Many student athletes don't even continue playing after college, and many of those who do will fail to reach the Major Leagues.[109]

These real numbers should ease the pressure, but unfortunately, they don't seem to be doing so. I don't know how many times I have heard parents and or coaches talk about a "kid's soccer career," "high school scholarship," or "acting career." Careers? They are kids. Why can't they play for fun? For comradery? For the love of the game? For the love of the art? Remember the question I asked during our interview at the top of this chapter? Why are we expecting our kids to know the answer to a question that we ourselves couldn't answer at their age?

It doesn't matter if your kid isn't the stand-out soccer player or a violin prodigy ready to play at the Grand Ole Opry by age twelve. We must let our children make choices based on what motivates and inspires them, what makes them happy, and what makes them feel like they are contributing to the world.

Fortunately, more people besides me have noticed the issue and are already finding solutions. This unhealthy drive for excessive achievement has our top education experts building programs to help kids, parents, and educators reduce academic and extracurricular pressure and create a more balanced life for each child. For example, Harvard's Graduate School of Education launched the Making Caring Common project in 2018.[110] That same year, Stanford University launched Challenge Success.[111] Both of these programs have resources available online.

As for me, I prefer not to call leaving an activity "quitting" but instead "changing course." I've always told my boys to follow their hearts and not to worry about disappointing me or their dad. We will always support their journey if they always try their best. We want to give them the flexibility to figure things out for themselves. So when they come to us with a possible "change of course," we ask them to think about why they want to make the change, but most importantly, about what *they* are going to do to make the change. How are they going to move through this slight correction? What is their plan of action?

I'll give you an example of how that usually goes. When Asher was seven, he decided that, after only playing a couple of seasons, he just didn't want to play baseball anymore. He was done. At seven years old.

My husband was not happy. He really wanted Asher to play. But Asher said his passion was soccer. We figured that this decision was probably based on the fact that, at the time, he was better at soccer than at baseball. We allowed him to make his decision, letting him know that we supported him, that it's okay to take a break, to change course—but also that it would be okay if he felt differently next season. Just because you're out this season doesn't mean you have to be out forever. And he felt good about his decision to play soccer instead of baseball. All was okay in the world.

Fast forward to the next season, when my husband was in the process of signing up Jackson for baseball. We decided to ask Asher whether he would like to play too. He said he'd think about it, and he did. After a few days, Asher announced during a conversation with Jackson that he would be playing baseball again. That was that. He was back in and changing course. At time of writing, he plays both soccer and baseball, but baseball is now his favorite sport. I'm so glad we gave him the confidence to tell us he didn't want to play when he did. He then came to like baseball again on his own, in his own time. And Jackson, who had at that time declared baseball his passion, has switched to golf at the age of twelve. Who knows what either of them will be interested in doing in a year from now? It doesn't matter to me.

Here's what I'm getting at: your children's passions are a moving target, likely to change at any given time. So give them the freedom to make their own choices about what they want to do rather than pressuring them to do what you *think* they should do, especially if it's something they're ready to move on from. Provide them with opportunities to figure out what drives them. Create an environment where they feel safe and secure in making decisions based on what their hearts are telling them. It's just part of the process, part of the journey, part of the unfolding. As for me, I am excited to see what catches Asher's and Jackson's eyes next.

Pro Parenting Tips: Trust Your Child's Choices

- Take care with how you talk about what your child is doing. Remember: "quitting" versus "changing course."
- Expose your child to all types of extracurriculars and allow her to choose between them. Listening more than you talk is good practice for compassion.
- Set reasonable boundaries around when it's appropriate for your child to decide, versus when you as the parent

should have the final word. For example, you could have a rule about no stopping in the middle of the season.

- Stay on top of the latest research and educational best practices: check out the websites for Challenge Success (http://www.challengesuccess.org/) and Making Caring Common (https://mcc.gse.harvard.edu/).
- Believe and know that your child is exactly where he should be at this moment in time.

The Path toward Leadership

In 2018, I put on an event through my nonprofit, Caring Counts. One of the speakers was a remarkable young girl named Natalie Hampton. Natalie spoke for about thirty minutes about how she was horribly bullied in elementary school. She described, in a way appropriate to elementary school and high school kids, how those bullies had hurt her deep inside. Parents and kids were sitting on the edge of their seats, feeling her pain, many with tears in their eyes.

Sadly, stories of bullying are common in our society. But what I want to focus on here is how Natalie emerged from this experience and became a global leader in the fight against bullying.

Natalie looked at this difficult time in her life and found a passion that drove her to help others. One way she has helped victims of bullying is by creating an app called Sit With Us that promotes a sense of belonging. This app is simple. If you are eating lunch alone at school, you can log onto this app and find someone to sit with in your school community. It's now used in schools all over the United States.

I've just talked about exposing children to all types of activities, experiences, places, and people. One of the benefits of that exposure can be teaching your children leadership skills. But how might you expose young children to leadership opportunities? Have no fear: your budding leader doesn't have to emerge because of a difficult life event. Still, you'll see how the skills Natalie used to become a leader can be taught by parents at home, skills like problem solving, empathy, and speaking up. You can mix lessons into your everyday parenting on a smaller, less traumatic scale that will teach your kids just those sorts of skills.

Studies show that the path to leadership begins early in life as a young person builds relationships and gains life experiences, and leadership traits often coalesce as children reach adolescence.[112]

There are so many ways to describe a leader. Interestingly, as I've researched leadership in children, a lot of the key traits are the same attributes I introduce to you throughout this book: resilience, empathy, self-awareness, creativity, curiosity, integrity, and listening skills, among others. Another key trait—in any context, not just leadership—is self-regulation, a term defined in a University of Michigan study as "a person's ability to control their thoughts, emotions, and actions to achieve a desired outcome."[113]

You don't often find the word "leadership" in early learning standards, but in many states in the United States, the idea still informs social-emotional learning outcomes, visible in key phrases like "self-confidence," "problem solving," "pro-social," and "makes independent decisions and choices."[114] For example, the social-emotional section of Pennsylvania's Pre-Kindergarten Early Learning Standards includes "know and state independent thoughts and feelings" and "participate in new experiences with confidence and independence."[115]

One way children at Laurence Elementary School learn about leadership is through the "solve and evolve" curriculum. This curriculum prompts children to look at a problem, think of ways to solve it, and evolve themselves in the process. If a child is feeling left out at recess, a teacher might ask a second child to help include the first child by asking, "What do you think you can do to help?" The second child can then state a few ideas, figure out which one he would like to use, and attempt to reach out to the child who is feeling bad. It sounds so simple, but it works. It gives children the ability to problem solve, and leaders must be problem solvers.

In addition to the lessons your children encounter at school—I'd like to introduce positive peer pressure into the mix as a way of teaching leadership. (Yes, peer pressure can be *positive*.) Leaders need to be comfortable in a group, including a group of other leaders. They also need to be able to discern which kinds of people they ought to socialize with. Educational experts at Penn State University say that "teaching children how to be a leader at a young age will help children deal with peer pressure in the teenage years. Being a leader is not an exact science, but teaching children the skills needed to be leaders [is] important to help prepare the next generation to take the lead and become responsible adults."[116]

I believe, as a teacher and a mother, that it's in our hands to help our children learn to choose, spend time with, and listen to peers who will exert that sort of positive influence on them. Here's how to help your kid find the leaders among her peers:

- Start talking early on: It's never too early to talk to your kids about peer pressure. Go through different scenarios that are age appropriate and talk about potential methods of handling them.
- Know all your children's friends: Know their names and have an open line of communication with their parents or guardians.
- Check potential peers' values: Ask, "Do the people you want to be friends with have values that are in line with yours? Are they interested in helping the world become better?"
- The power of "No": I've already talked about this. Kids need to learn to say no, something many adults struggle with. If you give your child the ability to say no when he needs to, this will show him that he can make his own decisions, including saying no to negative peer pressure and yes to positive peer pressure.
- Affirm good choices: When you see your child engaging in positive peer interactions, point it out and let her know you are proud of her

and that she should be proud of herself.

So say your child is already developing leadership skills and characteristics. The next step is to help your child find opportunities to put those skills into practice. At school, teachers often build responsibilities that involve taking on leadership roles into the classroom experience, such as line leaders, office attendants, student council members, and everything in between.

Most importantly, we can give our children leadership opportunities at home. This is where encouragement and, as I like to call it, the "gentle nudge" come in. The gentle nudge means that, instead of telling your child what to do, you lead your child to those positive skills I've talked about through soft suggestions and leading questions, gently nudging them toward leadership. I see leadership as more of a state of being than a specific role in a single moment in time. Leadership can take many forms throughout the day, in simple tasks. Asking an older kid to help watch a younger sibling is building a leader. Teaching your child to give to others is building a leader. So is providing the space for your child to find what excites her, so she can find a leadership role in her passion, such as being team captain for her favorite sport. Leadership is everywhere in life.

Finally, if you want your child to be a leader, model it. Are you a good leader, in the home or out of it? Do you listen to your kids' ideas and allow them to figure out their own problems when possible? How do you engage with the world as a leader?

The path toward leadership is a lifelong journey, a path you can lead your child along. You can help your child on this path.

Leadership skills allow children to have control of their lives and the ability to make things happen. Leadership instills confidence in themselves and trust in those around them. It helps children solve problems creatively and work in a team. Perhaps, like Natalie, it helps children become a positive force in the world. Leadership is a part of life. Leadership is for everyone.

Pro Parenting Tips: Teaching Leadership Skills

If you're feeling overwhelmed about creating leadership opportunities in your home, consider these focal points:

- Kids are most active in their passions. Where does your child shine? Look for leadership roles in that area.
- Teach your child to be a giver. Empathy is one of the most important traits in life and in building leaders.
- Help your child develop his voice. Be gentle and don't force what you think a leader should be; instead, find out how your child wants to express her leadership skills in the world.
- Teach your child how to say sorry and how to forgive. Encourage her to be a compassionate listener.
- Encourage connections with friends who are a positive influence.
- Expect that your child has the capacity to be a leader, no matter what his personality is.

Compare No More!: Trusting Yourself as a Parent

I've spent most of this chapter talking about how and when you need to trust your child. But learning to trust yourself as a parent—to really *believe* that when the chips are down, you'll make the best decision you can with the information and abilities you have—is just as important. When you feel that you can trust the process, trust the parenting instincts inside of you, even if the outside world or societal pressures are telling you something different, it can give you and your child the freedom to exist as you are.

That's the ideal, but the sheer volume of opinions out there can really make trusting yourself difficult. The early parenthood years are exhausting and frightening. Sometimes it feels like an unending stream of emotional lows and second guessing. And with the onslaught of social media groups and blog posts on parenting—"This way is best," "That way is wrong," "Don't *ever* do that"—a new parent, or an old one, can quickly lose self-confidence. That's definitely happened to me more than once.

Here's an example. In short, I had the worst time breastfeeding. The responsibility of feeding my child felt like a huge weight on my shoulders. It hurt so much, and my milk production was nowhere near what my baby Jackie needed. My lactation specialist urged me on: "This is the most beautiful thing you can do for your baby. This is how you bond." But it just wasn't happening.

So basically, I thought, *if I don't breastfeed, I'm hurting my child, myself, and our relationship.*

I felt like a failure. I felt unable, incompetent, and alone. Hmmmm… Welcome to parenthood.

Newsflash: This lack of trust in myself did not feel good. And it led me to worry more about my boys and whether they were getting everything they should from me and my husband. I have talked to countless parents who have felt the same way, insecure and unsure whether they were doing this parenting thing right. There's a lot of information and opinions out there, and there's no getting around the comparisons. When you're forced to look at the way everyone else is doing parenting, it can get too easy to compare ourselves unfairly.

As adults, we try to "keep up with the Joneses," our way of comparing each other with the rest of the world. But moments like these are where you must reset and trust in yourself and your ability to figure out what you need to do for yourself and your children. You won't be perfect in your parenting choices—no one is—but you can trust that you will do enough, that you *are* enough, for your children. Deepak

Chopra says, "Do you love yourself just as you are? . . . Well-loved children absorb from their parents a sense of self-worth that lasts a lifetime."[117] For when you're in your low moments, here is a list of ways to help you (and your children) be kind and compassionate to yourself and love yourself just as you are, even when the world seems to be telling you the opposite:

- Smile at your reflection in the mirror.
- Let others compliment you.
- Bask in other people's approval when it comes your way.
- Be gentle with yourself over small mistakes.
- Value who you are and stand up for yourself.
- Get to know yourself like a friend.
- Be easy about your personal quirks.
- Be as natural as possible, not worrying if you are pleasing or displeasing others.
- Speak your truth when you know you should.[118]

So, as much as you can, compare no more! Remind yourself, repeatedly, that it serves no beneficial purpose. Kids hear us. Kids listen. Let's make sure they hear positivity, and that they feel seen and understood for who they are—for what makes them special and unique.

In addition to comparing yourself unfairly to others, it's also vital to avoid comparing your children to each other (or to other children). It's just not helpful, and it creates unnecessary fear and anxiety for you and your child. When you notice yourself comparing your child to a "normal standard," trust the research available to you to know when you should be taking action and when you should let your child develop at her own pace and exist in her own space.

I admit that I compared my kids when they were smaller. I compared them in my mind and when talking with family and friends. I knew I was doing it, but I kept on doing it. I couldn't help it. Jackson and Asher are almost exactly a year apart, so it was easy to see what each of them was doing, almost side by side. Adding to the ease of comparison was the fact that I journaled to each of them every month. When I did that, I could easily look back and see what Jackson had done in comparison to Asher at the same time, just a year before. I watched all the developmental milestones: first smiles, first steps—first anything. I did it because I wanted to make sure they were on track, that they were healthy, and that, if I saw anything that didn't seem right, I could get them what they needed ASAP. For one, I knew that around one in sixty-eight American children are on the autism spectrum, and that all the research indicates that the sooner you diagnose it, the sooner you can begin the work to help your child.[119] So I made sure I knew the signs so I could change the trajectory of my children's development—if the diagnosis occurred. Looking back at those journals now, I can see just how much I watched what they were doing. Here's a little sample from Asher's journal:

September 10, 2009

Dear Asher,

You are now nearly eight months old, and you are so, so cute. You smile all the time. You are now crawling and CLIMBING on everything. I call you my little "Dare Devil." We must watch your every move. You scratched your eye trying to get out of your crib. You are going to walk early, we think, because you can get up on your own and stand. And last night, for the first time, you ate the same dinner we all did. You had chicken, rice, and avocado! You love avocado!

I love you so!

Mommy

And here's my journal entry to Jackson on the very same day:

Dear Jackson,

Wow, you can talk! Mommy and Daddy figured out that you have at least a 300-word vocabulary. We wrote down the words you know. You are a great communicator. You are going to be starting school soon; Mommy and Me!

You love Thomas the Train and all of his friends. You
continue to love to play golf too!
Love you with all my heart!
Mommy

And so there you have it. I was tracking everything I could. Smiles, check. Standing, check. Vocabulary, check. From there, I went on to make sure Asher was on track with Jackson. And if Asher was ahead of Jackson, I wanted to make sure Jackson was okay. But as I grew as a mother and felt more confident in the fact that all would be fine, I was able to let go of the comparison, just a little.

And here's where the lightbulb finally goes off in my brain: I don't want anyone comparing *me* to anyone else, so why oh why would I compare my children to each other, or with any other kid for that matter? It just doesn't make sense. It serves no purpose. And according to research, comparing siblings can even have a negative impact on a child's self-worth.

In a study from Brigham Young University, researchers found that "it's hard for parents to not notice or think about differences between their children. It's only natural."[120] But "parents' beliefs about their children, not just their actual parenting, may influence who their children become."[121] To help children succeed, parents should instead be looking at each child's unique strengths.

Trust the parenting path, trust the innate well-being of your children, and trust yourself as a parent. In particular, trust yourself to know your kid better than anyone else in this world. You are doing all you can, right now in this moment in time, to create the castle of your dreams and the best environment for your kids.

Pro Parenting Tips: Ditching Comparison

- Keep a parenting journal to (1) keep track of milestones for doctors and (2) remember those precious moments.

- Track developmental milestones, but don't worry if your child isn't "up to speed" in comparison to others. Instead, enjoy them as they come. (For education on developmental milestones, go to the CDC's website on the topic.[122]).

- Celebrate your child's individuality, and help him celebrate himself with simple mantras like "I am loved," "I am kind," etc.

- Celebrate differences. Expose your child to people different from herself and explore what makes those people unique in the world.

- Love your child *unconditionally*. Love him no matter what. (There are more details on that coming up in the very next chapter!)

Chapter 5:

Love

What can you do to promote world peace?
Go home and love your family.

—Mother Teresa

Love is the bedrock of your family castle. Now it might seem at first as though love and compassion are the same thing—or at least very similar in meaning. But there is a difference. Compassion is sympathy for and desire to help alleviate the suffering of others. In contrast, love is a deep feeling of affection and attachment toward someone. Compassion does not need love to exist. But where love is, compassion will absolutely be present.

Children need and want love from their parents. They are aware of whether and how much they are loved, and they cherish love when they receive it. To illustrate this, I wanted to share with you a poem Jackson wrote for a school assignment:

Family Love

by Jackson Bunnin, age eleven

I remember the tenderness in the room

Everyone understood that we all were filled with bliss

not because of the gifts, but

because of the happiness that we were blessed with

When we handed out the vibrantly colored boxes

We all felt delighted and ecstatic

the way you feel

when you know you are cherished and cared for
Togetherness is something to be embraced
and not pushed away
It is an important, valuable thing
that can be hard to hold for many people
What our world needs to realize
is that there is so much more to happiness than material things
and that people can make you feel needed
and that people will make you feel satisfied
There is only one word to capture this scene
Family Love

Love in Childhood

Parental warmth will impact your child's well-being now and through adulthood. Research and anecdotal evidence show that family love can have a big impact on our emotional well-being. That impact can be either positive or negative and affect our emotions and behaviors. A recent study out of Harvard has found that people who had loving parents in childhood have better lives later. The study measured parental warmth, affection, and love in childhood, and then measured factors of mid-life flourishing ("such as happiness, self-acceptance, social relationships and being more likely to contribute to the community").[123] This was true even when the study controlled for socioeconomic and other factors. The association is clear and consistent. People who remember their parents as warm and loving are flourishing at much higher rates in adulthood. Study director Tyler VanderWeele says, "We see that parental warmth led to more happiness and social acceptance, as well as less depression, anxiety and drug use."[124]

This study can be used as a practical tool when parenting. It gives us proof that loving our kids and showing them affection really does matter, now and in the future, and it's something we all can do every day. Friedrich Nietzsche once said, "In family life, love is the oil that eases friction, the cement that binds closer together, and the music that brings harmony."

Dr. Mary Elizabeth Dean is an educator with over ten years of experience as a teacher and curriculum leader. While it might seem that loving your children is an instinct that doesn't need cultivation, Dr. Dean explains family love as a developmental process: "Healthy family love is a choice that starts with the parents. It isn't something that happens without thought and dedication. There are several ways to build healthy family love throughout the lifespan of the family. . . . By being a responsive caregiver, you can start the secure attachment that research has shown leads to higher social functioning later in life. Along with better mental and physical health, a secure attachment gives your child a greater capacity to form healthy attachments with others."[125]

Along the same lines, a Harvard longitudinal study surveying a sample of eighty-one men found that "warmer relationships with parents in childhood predict greater security of attachment to intimate partners in late life, and that this link is mediated in part by the degree to which individuals in midlife rely on emotion-regulatory styles that facilitate or inhibit close relationship connections."[126] These findings highlight how childhood environments can impact individuals even as adults.

The Importance of Self-Love

So purposefully constructing love in your family is essential. How do you do it? Well, self-love is one of the most important steps on your parenting path. It may sound a bit counterintuitive, especially for new parents hyper-focused on their children, but it's not. And I'm not talking about what we see all over the internet: #selflove, #selfcare, a picture of a mom lying out by the waves with a "sex on the beach" cocktail in hand. Yes, that's a form of self-care. Vacations are good. I'm all for vacations! But before you can love your children—and teach them to love themselves—you *must* learn to love yourself. I've had to learn this lesson myself multiple times, and I'm still learning. Over the years, as I have studied, researched, and had on-the-job training as a real-life mom, I've developed a certain level of self-confidence, but confident doesn't necessarily mean self-loving. A key element of learning to love yourself is figuring out where you came from, including what experiences you had in childhood are driving you—as a person and as a parent.

Near the midpoint of writing this book, before I had put it out into the world of book agents and publishers, I stopped writing it. I chose to then because life had just become too busy, but I look back now and know this pause was meant to be because, even with all my good intentions, I still felt a lack in myself and my parenting. Some things I was doing just didn't feel right, and I needed to dig into myself to figure out why. But I just didn't know how to.

Enter Suzanne Morris, licensed medical assistant and associate certified coach, who helped me realize that, in some ways, I parented based on how I was parented. As a child, I had internalized my parents' strategies and unconsciously implemented some of them in my own family. As Suzanne told me when I interviewed her again for this book, "we all have a child that lives inside of us that is alive and well, the inner self—and that child is often driving the bus even through adulthood."[127]

I'll be clear, my parents were great, and they did the best they could, but there were differences between how they parented me and how I want to parent my own children. The cool thing is that Suzanne and I didn't take years and years of therapy to figure those differences out. In fact, we were able to sort me out relatively quickly. I've included Suzanne's research here to help you sort yourself out too.

In addition to her education, Suzanne's work is based on more than twenty thousand hours spent sitting with clients and seeing what really influences people and their behaviors. Suzanne quickly learned she had to help parents move forward, but in order to not be tied to their younger selves, they had to understand what formative experiences have really shaped them to be who they currently are. It really speaks to a quote from George Santayana, a philosopher, essayist, poet, and novelist who said, "Those who cannot remember the past are condemned to repeat it."[128] She observed a repeated pattern that she describes this way: "We are all shaped by what we see and hear. Much of this shaping occurred at a very young age while we were developing. We formed what I like to call an Operating System. This is our blueprint and the place we navigate our lives from. It is the motherboard of all of our desires, motivations, responses, reactions, and navigations. They all originate from this Operating System. If we can have an awareness of what has created our Operating Systems, we can choose to release what is not working."[129]

She explained to me once that "if someone had a disconnect at seven, [then] as they were talking to me right now, I could see it come over them physically and energetically in that moment—they looked seven years old, and they sounded seven years old. I had this realization early on in my work. We all develop an operating system, and just like a computer, it is on our hard drive. It stays with us for the rest of our lives unless we reset it."[130]

In the same way you can affect your children's operating systems, your parents have affected yours. In order to help that effect be for a child's good, Suzanne says that it's vital for children to not be invisible. To help children to really feel seen and heard, Suzanne says it all really starts with "Birthrights" (or the needs all children require for healthy development), of which she identifies five:

1. Unconditional love, the first emotion a parent has for a child, allowing him to know that he is loved no matter what.
2. Safety and security, both physical and emotional.
3. Attention and acceptance, felt through affirmations like "I see you," "I value you," and "I respect your individuality."
4. Nurturing behaviors, such as understanding, supporting, praise, and warmth in both trials and victories.

5. Teaching healthy boundaries for discipline, fairness, and patience through good examples.

Now here's where it gets interesting. Suzanne says that "if you didn't get one of the Birthright needs met, you do one of two things: You create a behavior that will eventually get that birthright need fulfilled or you overcompensate for the lack of receiving it and get the need met for yourself. Both methods turn into a survival behavior. . . . In most cases we don't know how to do something that wasn't taught to us, so it becomes generational. If I'm born into a family that doesn't know how to communicate and learn that feelings are okay and that I can express and work through these things and have communication with my inner self, then I have a child and I don't know how to not only give that to myself but then to my child." This is how we pass it on from one generation to the next generation.

Suzanne says in her book:

> It can be difficult knowing and learning how to do something that we were not taught. If something was never modeled for us or given to us, chances are we might struggle knowing how to give these things to ourselves now. Sometimes, we may even block others from giving us these things because we simply do not have any experience of accepting them. It may feel so foreign we might not believe that we are worthy to receive them. Often, we overcompensate in an area to feel the safety we did not receive, or to prove our value and worth to ourselves. We also create behaviors to get these needs met from the outside. These are Survival Behaviors. If you are living in some sort of survival it means that you have created a way to get these needs met by doing something to ensure the result.[131]

I'll pass on this story Suzanne told me about herself. Suzanne was hardwired differently from her mother, who just didn't have an understanding of her sensitivity or the time to develop one. When Suzanne was a child, she was always told that she was difficult. Now she knows she was just sensitive, but it took well into her twenties for her to understand that.

What Suzanne told me next is so interesting to me. Her son happens to be just like Suzanne—sensitive. She said if she hadn't figured out what she was missing in her operating system and made peace with it, she would have passed this sort of treatment down to her own son, who would have been unable to fully express his needs as a sensitive soul.

In some ways, Suzanne's case makes total sense. She had to learn survival skills to live in a world where she was "difficult," and she did so by learning how to "handle" everyone and everything. She did survive for a long time that way, but she was not being true to who she was, and she wasn't able to function in the world as her true self. Hearing that was a big lightbulb moment for me.

If you are concerned that your operating system has been affected for the worse, don't worry. There is no time that you cannot begin this work. You can always do this. Suzanne suggests starting with the above birthrights and working your way back through your memories. "It's a way to shift out of survival behaviors and move forward."

First, find a quiet place to sit and remember for a few minutes. Ask yourself, "Hey, what did I get? What things didn't I get?"

Allow yourself an awareness of what happened to you and feel the emotions that come. Suzanne shared this exercise with me:

- Find a photo of yourself that really connects you to that child you used to be and that inner child that is still you.
- Find the love and compassion you feel for that child and then allow that child to get angry. You do not need to call your parents and tell them you are angry, but being angry means you are an adult acknowledging and validating this child's feelings. This is the process of reparenting yourself.
- Affirm to yourself, "You are right. You did not get these things, and

I'm sorry. You can be angry." Allow your inner self to be angry and hold those emotions. "You have to hold the space to let your inner self feel it again," says Suzanne.

- Once you have allowed your inner child to feel this anger, it will dissipate. You will feel heard; your inner self will feel heard.

What happens when you begin this process is that you start to develop compassion for your parents. Do you recall the distinction between love and compassion at the top of this chapter? They don't often align in life outside of the necessarily limited number of your family and close friends, but here the two concepts can coexist. You can think about what your parents were going through at the time. Was it difficult for them to be parents? Perhaps they were trying to create this wonderful family while thinking they kept falling short, just like you.

Suzanne told me, "This opens the door for compassion in the family and compassion for yourself, and that broadens the family experience. This is not a perfect family, but a better one and happier one. The relationship with ourselves—truly loving ourselves and being compassionate with ourselves—has to come before anyone or anything else, because when we are hard on ourselves because of the survival behavior we developed, it becomes our internal critical parent." Suzanne calls this internal critic the "gatekeeper," the soldier that stands at the gate of you that makes sure you're going to be safe. It's your way of keeping yourself in line, safe, but when we are too critical to ourselves, self-compassion and self-love are lacking. This makes it difficult to be happy, loving, and compassionate to our children, which makes it difficult for us to teach them those behaviors in turn. If you aren't treating yourself well and with compassion, your children are seeing and absorbing this pattern and developing their own stern "gatekeeper" that will limit their growth.

The fact of the matter is that there is a beautiful little child inside all of us, our true self that either gets nurtured or smashed in childhood.

As a parent, you must have compassion for yourself and really think about that little child inside of you. That doesn't mean that you should stop trying. "In being compassionate with myself, it doesn't mean that I don't hold myself accountable," Suzanne says. Rather, that inner understanding is key to navigating your own inner world and the world around you. It will teach you self-compassion and self-love that are essential to your emotional health as an inner child, an adult child to your parents, and a parent in your own right. Suzanne says that we can develop a new part of ourselves she calls "The Aligned Inner Parent," to help nurture ourselves and then our children.

Suzanne helped me along my own parenting path. I am still far from perfect, but I feel solid in my decisions and much more aware in my role as a parent and as an individual. Here's one last nugget of advice from Suzanne that I adore: Name your inner child. I did it when she asked me, and I have come back to this idea again and again. My inner child is named "Joy." Any time I feel a shift or split from myself, my *real* self, I try my best to go back to Joy. It's going to take time and practice to succeed in loving yourself—really loving yourself, every single part—but just being aware gives you a huge leg up. I know you can change your operating system for the better and learn to teach your kids to love themselves too, from where you are right now.

Pro Parenting Tips: Getting Acquainted with Your Inner Self

- Take care of yourself, physically, mentally, and spiritually.
- Give yourself the gift of acceptance.
- Seek education in learning how to bring peace and love to yourself.
- Provide yourself with positive routines in your own life.

Teaching Your Children Self-Love

Now let's move toward how to teach your children self-love. We've already talked a lot in this book about the importance of modeling behaviors for your children, and we've talked about how you can model self-love in this very chapter. But there's also another method of teaching self-love that I'd like to share with you here. It's probably not what you think.

I begin with one of my all-time favorite parenting experts in the world and one of my greatest mentors, Dr. Michele Borba. Dr. Borba is known globally for her work as an educational psychologist and author of twenty-five parenting books, including the best seller *UnSelfie* and her latest book (a must read!), *Thrivers: The Surprising Reasons Why Some Kids Struggle and Others Shine.* I had the opportunity to interview Dr. Borba for my podcast, *Kids under Construction*, in September 2020.[132] One of the many things she shared with me is precisely what this chapter speaks to: how to inspire your child to fall in love with life and herself by helping her find her passion. She explains why doing so is not just some frivolous expectation in the world of parenting. In fact, it is foundational to building a successful and well-balanced child and adult.

To support this assertion, Dr. Borba told me about the work of one of *her* favorite parenting experts and mentors, Dr. Emmy Werner. (You feel the circle of love here?) Dr. Werner wanted to find out why some kids struggle and others don't. So, she began a longitudinal study where she tracked the same kids for four decades.[133]

Dr. Borba explained that "about halfway through the study, Dr. Werner [realized she] kept seeing specific commonalities. Number one is that successful kids had connections with people; relationships and empathy were cultivated. Number two, these successful kids had coping skills—that is, someone had taught them how to cope . . . mindfulness or deep breathing, something. And the third thing she discovered is that they all had a hobby that drove their passion."

According to Dr. Borba, that hobby or passion, whether it be woodworking, knitting, baseball, dancing, or books, was something the children continued to use for the rest of their lives. And the silver lining in all of this was that when the children experienced adversity, they went back to their passion where they had found their love of life and self-love. Doing so helped center them and gave them hope.

On that note, Dr. Borba says that now is the time to help your child find her passion—now, now, *now*. Embrace everything that inspires your child. Everything, you might ask? Yes, wherever you see her love of life and love and appreciation of self, show up and be present. And remember that your child's interests will be fluid: hobbies and passions change and evolve. We are never done learning, growing, or exploring.

This can be quite easy to do. Just watch your child and see what he likes. If you've got a budding artist, find ways for him to express himself through art. Here's an example: Jackson is very creative. I call him "my little creator." So, when Valentine's Day rolled around during his kindergarten year, I asked him if he'd like to make homemade Valentine cards. He was into it and spent hours making a Valentine prototype. His little six-year-old creativity came up with an elephant blowing heart kisses out into the world, with a tiny green bird sitting atop the elephant tweeting out hearts! Then we reproduced copies for him to take to his classmates. Doing that was my way of showing my child I was there to help him enjoy and develop his passion. You can do the same.

Remember, as your child is developing whatever her hobby of choice is, she's also developing love of self. Dr. Jade Wu, also known as The Savvy Psychologist, says, "One of the greatest ways you can love yourself is to give yourself the satisfaction of mastery and freedom of expression."[134]

It doesn't matter what form that expression takes. All that matters is that it's what your child cares about. Dr. Wu says, "Humans are restless, creative creatures. We simply need to express ourselves. You may not think of yourself as creative because you've never taken painting lessons or been confident with a piano, but not all creativity fits into the box of traditional arts. Maybe you're the dinner party comedian who cracks people up. Or you've always got the best Halloween costume. . . . Perhaps your dream is to run a marathon on every continent."[135] (Or, as you'll see in the next few paragraphs, it could be collecting sports cards.) Simply help your child find what he loves—what he is passionate about—and see how he begins to love himself more and more. Inspire quite literally means "in-spirit." In the words of Dr. Wayne Dyer, "when you are inspired by something, it means that you are living in line with your spirit."[136] So help your child listen to her spirit, to the whispers of her heart and soul. Here are a couple of stories about children and parents who did just that.

Adam's Story: A Passion for Sports Cards

Here's passion in play in the summer of 2020, a summer that was difficult for so many children. Twelve-year-old Adam had recently proclaimed his newest passion: collecting sports cards and memorabilia, including dreams of a business of his own.

"Great," said his mom. "I'm happy for him, but at the same time I realize he is only twelve. I know that passions can develop, strengthen, change, go off track, go back on track, or something in the middle for a period. . . . Passions can be fluid. But as his parent, when he told me of his newest passion, I was supportive and ready to help in any way he asked or needed."[137]

Part of this new passion is the love Adam has for the guy who introduced him to all of this: Tim, a family friend who owns his own sports card and memorabilia collection business. Adam visits the shop regularly, and the two of them talk for hours about cards. Sometimes they trade, and sometimes Tim shows Adam the reality of life—and doesn't budge on the negotiation.

One weekend when Adam went to visit Tim after attending a card show, Adam told Tim that he had used his savvy and knowledge to make one of his best trades ever. Tim promptly acknowledged Adam's business acumen and surprised him with a pack of basketball cards.

As these two shared their passion for cards and business and Tim filled the role of friend and mentor, Adam's passion and love of self and life were inspired.

James's Story: A Passion for Golf

Speaking of mentors, I love learning from coaches. These fantastic mentors really energize their athletes as they share their expertise. As I've said elsewhere in this book, my son Jackson plays golf. He loves the game. He also loves his golf coach, James, who in my eyes is a five-star, first-rate inspirer of kids' passions. One day during practice, Coach James and I got to talking about that very topic.

James has been a golf pro and coach his entire life. He said when he was in high school, he witnessed an interaction between his own coach and another golfer. According to James, that young high school golfer was exceptional (he was headed to Clemson, one of the best golf programs at the time), and he was just starting out with this new coach.

During one of the practices, the amazing golfer made a big mistake on the driving range and began pounding his club into the ground repeatedly. James stayed on track with his own practice, but as he watched in a covert manner, he saw his coach go up to the distraught young golfer and gently put his arm around him. The coach told the kid that he wasn't good enough of a player to pound the golf club into the grass; nor was any pro golfer on the PGA tour. The kid looked as confused as James said he felt. The coach went on to say, "You can't ever do that again if you want me to be your coach. You must be your best friend. As your coach, I'm rooting for you. Your parents are rooting for you, but if you're not on your side, there's no way you can develop your game, your passion." And clearly, the young golfer was hurting himself. He wasn't loving himself.

The coach repeated himself, just as calmly: "You must be your best friend. If you are too hard on yourself and don't move through your distractions or difficult periods, you just can't do it with only me and your parents. Be your best friend."

That conversation was a lesson that has stayed with James his entire life. And he passed it on to his own children, four of them, who are all successful and thriving in the world.

Taking Passions to the Next Level . . . Or Maybe Not

"Be your best friend" is now one of my go-to teaching phrases when I see my boys learning and evolving in their hobbies and passions. A child must love himself as he would expect a best friend to love him.

As you read in Adam's and James's stories, outside mentors have a unique way of inspiring our kids toward their passions. Utilize those people, especially when you find yourself struggling in that realm. Dr. Borba explains, for your kids' growth, if you can't do it, "find someone who can." You can achieve this by, first, asking your child if she knows someone she'd like to work with and learn from. Then ask fellow parents and teachers for recommendations, or just do good old-fashioned research on the internet. Find those experts in your community. Soon you'll find mentors suited for your child who will help inspire your child's passion and in turn his self-love. Welcome those mentors into the fold and then put effort into growing those relationships.

Joani Geltman is an expert in child development and parenting with thirty years of experience. She has also raised a successful, healthy, and happy daughter, an actress who has appeared on Broadway and in several movies. Geltman explained to me that she did not push her daughter; she only supported what her daughter wanted to do. When they started out, she says, "it was not sophisticated at all," and she adds that if you want your children to find their passions, it must happen in a "natural way."[138]

Remember in chapter 4 where I talked about letting kids "change course" with extracurriculars? Those principles apply equally as well here because we want our kids to become who *they* want to become, who *they* are being called to be.

Pro Parenting Tips: Raising Passionate Children

Here are some tips from Geltman:

- Let your child develop his own passions, at his own pace.
- Watch what your child likes to do. Ask your child about her interests.
- Allow your child to be who he is, not who you want him to be.
- Remember the lessons from chapter 4! Passion doesn't always have to have an end result. It can simply be for enjoyment.

And some tips from me:

- Encourage time with friends and mentors. Kids learn new things from others all the time.
- Offer many opportunities and give your child the space and time to explore. Don't get stuck with just one.
- Model your own passions: Show your kids what inspires you! Share your passions with your child.
- Allow your child the process of discovery through compassion. Let her discover what is in her heart, her soul, her spirit.
- Accept that your child will have lots of different passions as he grows. Many adults are still searching for that certain thing that resonates with them.

The Foundation of Family Love

As I close this chapter, here's a real-life story that may speak to you. After Kent Pekel, a father of three, lost his young wife to cancer, he truly realized the importance of family love and warmth. As Pekel worked to parent his three small children alone, his life was changed by a piece of advice from a preschool teacher. She said, "From now on, it all depends on the relationships—your relationships with those three kids. The relationship is a thing."[139] (Here's to all the preschool teachers out there!)

This advice led Pekel on a life's journey to find out how parents can develop strong loving relationships with their kids. He is now an educator and president and CEO of the Search Institute, which "initiated research to understand how relationships shape youth success. The result was the Developmental Relationships Framework, which includes five essential elements and 20 corresponding actions to strengthen relationships with and between youth."[140]

I love the Developmental Relationships Framework. It's bursting with love, warmth, and helpful tips. Here are the elements and actions mentioned above (you may recognize some from elsewhere in this book!):

1. **Express Care:** Show me that I matter to you.
   a. Be dependable—Be someone I can trust.
   b. Listen—Really pay attention when we are together.
   c. Believe in me—Make me feel known and valued.
   d. Be warm—Show me you enjoy being with me.
   e. Encourage—Praise me for my efforts and achievements.
2. **Challenge Growth:** Push me to keep getting better.
   a. Expect my best—Expect me to live up to my potential.
   b. Stretch—Push me to go further.
   c. Hold me accountable—Insist I take responsibility for my actions.
   d. Reflect on failures—Help me learn from mistakes and setbacks.
3. **Provide Support:** Help me achieve tasks and complete goals.
   a. Navigate—Guide me through hard situations and systems.
   b. Empower—Build my confidence to take charge of my life.
   c. Advocate—Stand up for me when I need it.
   d. Set boundaries—Put in place limits that keep me on track.

4. **Share Power:** Treat me with respect and give me a say.
   a. Respect me—Take me seriously and treat me fairly.
   b. Include me—Involve me in decisions that affect me.
   c. Collaborate—Work with me to solve problems and reach goals.
   d. Let me lead—Create opportunities for me to take action and lead.

5. **Expand Possibilities:** Connect me with people and places that broaden my world.
   a. Inspire—Inspire me to see possibilities for my future.
   b. Broaden horizons—Expose me to new ideas, experiences, and places.
   c. Connect—Introduce me to people who can help me grow.[141]

Family love is truly the foundation for which we can begin to build our beautiful, unique castle. I am inspired by the way Michael J. Fox puts it; "Family is not an important thing. It's everything."[142] And as my son Asher explains it in his middle school essay application: "I really love my family because they are hands down the best people in the world. I love spending time with my mom, dad, and brother. We are the best family. I truly am grateful for my family."

How do you want to describe your family love? Imagine the extraordinary foundation you can build. I hope you found lots of inspiration here. I hope you can see with clarity that you have the power, right now, to build the castle of your dreams. In the end, love is something instinctive for parents, and when we struggle to prioritize love, whether for ourselves, our child, or our family, it's usually because something else is getting in the way, something you now have some of the tools to find and heal. Expectations are another of those possible obstacles, so we'll talk about those next.

Pro Parenting Tips: Building a Castle of Love

- As Dr. Dean explains, healthy family love is a choice you make. Choose it.
- Use the Developmental Relationships Framework to really work toward expressing care to your children.
- Be present: Just be there, even when it's inconvenient, even when it's messy.
- Use all components of the CASTLE Method:
  - » Compassion: everyday
  - » Acceptance: everyday
  - » Security: everyday
  - » Trust: everyday
  - » Love: everyday
  - » Expectations: everyday
  - » Education: everyday

Chapter 6:

Expectations

Become aware of your negative expectations and practice
replacing them with positive expectations.
—Debbie Ford

When I became a mother, I put up a very large chalkboard in my
newborn baby's nursery to use as a schedule board. To give it a little
charm, I even glued little wooden animals onto it that I had picked up
from a craft store. I wrote down feeding and napping times, planning
it all out to help me keep my schedule straight. (Can you say "sleep
deprivation"?)

As my children grew, schedules equaled less stress for both me and
them. Of course, we went off schedule many times, but that was okay.
Scheduling my kids' time is more about limiting chaos and letting
them know what is happening in their world. To this day, at ages twelve
and thirteen, they ask me, "Can you go over the schedule? What are
we doing today? Tomorrow?" As Jackson and Asher have grown, they
even like to recite the schedule for the family themselves. They enjoy
being the schedule keepers. Knowing what's expected of us throughout
the day gives all of us a sense of calm.

When we think about expectations, usually the definition in the dictionary suffices for practical purposes: "a strong belief that something
will happen or be the case in the future," or "a belief that someone will
or should achieve something."[143] But what do expectations mean when
it comes to parenting? A lot more than you might initially think, and
it's important to understand why.

Parental expectations can be both helpful and harmful to the development of a child. As I have discussed in previous chapters, teaching our children self-love, self-compassion, and self-acceptance is at the core of building a strong sense of identity. It allows your child to move through the world with confidence in himself. Teaching those things works best when combined with clear expectations on your part, but if those expectations are too many or too high, they can do more harm than good.

In this chapter, we'll look at some helpful expectations within family roles as well as how expectations of joy open up our world. Then we'll address the harmful expectations we sometimes place on ourselves and our children through a discussion of flexibility, including strategies for letting go of those harmful expectations.

Optimism, Involvement, and Celebrations: Helpful Expectations

As our children's leaders in the family, if we do not guide our children—in part by having expectations for them—they will feel the lack of structure and support. Helpful expectations also tell our children that what they do matters to us, which in turn grants them a profound sense of belonging.

Our positive expectations guide our children's development. Because we expect our children to walk, we will help guide that development, watching and gently helping them navigate those first steps. Because we expect our children to read, we begin reading to them as babies, even knowing that it will be years before they begin to identify letters.

Our expectations also help our children find their paths in life. If the expectation in your family is that you and your children are lifelong learners, education will naturally be a priority, and higher education is more likely (more about education in the next chapter). All of these things are positive expectations.

Expect Joy!: Optimism and Family Traditions

Now, expecting your children to do chores is a given, but expectations don't all have to be about the dull or mundane. In fact, even the most basic expectations will be a healthier experience for your child if you approach them in an optimistic way. Albert Einstein said, "Rejoice with your family in the beautiful land of life." Expectations can be joyful, and I mean that literally! You can expect joy in your daily life—and teach your kids to do so—by celebrating the positive.

I love celebrating! My mom did too, and I'm sure that's why I try to find ways to celebrate every single day as well as on special occasions and holidays. My family celebrates the big stuff and the little stuff, even the stuff we might take for granted, like being alive and the beautiful morning sunrise, and we love it, especially my kids! Exclamation points here! Might sound exhausting, but it's not. Why? It just depends on how you see joy. When I focus on all of the little sources of joy, the joy I find is endless. This next section is going to help you heighten your awareness and connect you to more joyful expectations. Think you're a pessimist? Not to worry. According to science, humankind is generally positively focused, so you're already predisposed to this expectation and all the benefits that come with it.

The Pollyanna Principle

The "Pollyanna Principle" is a scientific term referring to the human tendency for optimism—that is, that human beings are biologically predisposed to see the positive in life. Also called the "positivity bias," this trait was named after the main character of Eleanor H. Porter's book *Pollyanna*. Always cheerful, Pollyanna constantly plays the "Glad Game," which involves always trying to find at least one good thing in any situation, no matter how depressing. We all have the potential to be more like Pollyanna than we think.

Unfortunately, not everyone sees optimism as a good outlook on the world. You might have even heard "Pollyanna" used as an insult. I have often been called a Pollyanna in life, and I have even referred to myself as a Pollyanna (in a self-deprecating way) when talking to others outside of my immediate family, such as friends or colleagues, though it's always felt at odds with who I am deep inside. I was even unfollowed on social media once by a family member who said, "All you do is post about good things." *Really? You want me to post about negative things?* It didn't make sense then, and now I know my instinct has always served me well. If someone critiques you, let it go and move forward with confidence.

Of course, it is possible to be too optimistic, to dismiss negative emotions and give false assurances instead of empathy. In today's world, that is referred to as "toxic positivity." It is often well-intentioned but can cause alienation and a feeling of separation, so learn the signs and watch for it in yourself, particularly when interacting with your kids.

On the other end of the spectrum, it's impossible to be optimistic all the time. Psychologist Courtney E. Ackerman says, "We all have our down days and difficult moments, and none of us can be Pollyanna all the time. As with most things in life, the sweet spot is in a healthy balance of positivity and optimism along with realism, a sense of context, and a working understanding of what is appropriate and when."[144]

But even for those with clinical depression, there is hope. A study done in 1980 found that depression was negatively correlated with happiness, but not correlated at all with the ability to focus on the positive. Ackerman notes, "This indicates that our inherent positivity bias is something separate from the mood disorders that afflict so many of us and suggests that we are still capable of focusing on the positive even in the most trying and depressing times. Perhaps this innate tendency towards the positive is what the many treatments for depression are able to harness and reinforce, guiding us to use our own inner strength to restore a healthy balance of positivity and realism instead of falling on the negative side of the spectrum."[145]

So, based on all this evidence, why not start expecting joy? When you're feeling down on yourself, have faith that that innate positivity is there. In your better moments, take responsibility as a parent to build positivity in yourself and your children with concrete action. Dr.

Michele Borba gives a starting point: "Keep reminding your kids and yourself, 'We can do this.' Positive self-talk negates pessimism, reduces stress & opens hope. The key is to make sure your kid hears those messages enough, so he says it to himself & builds optimism."[146] Focus on positive thoughts, filtering out negative thoughts when you are able. Life is supposed to be fun and filled with joy. So, expect joy! You can be a Pollyanna whenever you are ready. It's all up to you. And your kids will thank you.

Expect Involvement: Family Chores

On a more concrete, actionable note, a great way to set positive and helpful expectations inside the home is to assign family chores. You can say to your kids, "We need your help to keep this family going," and as your children comply, they will feel a sense of belonging, that they are fulfilling their roles as members of the family who must do their part. Chores also grant opportunities to learn and practice life skills. You don't want to send your child off to college without knowing how to do her own laundry or cook for herself, right?

Now how you go about organizing chores in your home will be up to you. Here are a couple of questions to ask yourself: Will your children work on a rotating chore schedule or have a fixed set of tasks? Will they be paid for satisfactorily completing their chore assignments? If so, will it be in money, candy, or some other reward? Personally, I have decided not to pay my kids for chores because I want my children to see chores as an opportunity to help their family. We are all a part of this family, we all have a role in this family, and so we need to help each other—and we want to keep our castle clean and free of distractions. There are occasions when we do pay our boys for big projects they might be working on in the home, but that's done on a case-by-case basis.

Another essential question is how to determine what tasks are age appropriate for a given child. Pathways.org is a wonderful website with many free resources for early parenting. Here are some of their ideas for how to get kids involved in those very early years.[147]

Age-Appropriate Chores: 2–3 Years

- **Put the toys in the bin:** Telling your child "I bet I can put these away faster than you" will make the chore more of a game and more fun for your child. Cleaning up toys may allow your child to walk up and down stairs, or simply walk across the room with a toy in his hand, helping with their gross motor skills. He also has the chance to identify where things belong. Using a "clean up" song is also very helpful. This is a strategy many daycares/preschools use; use the same one your child hears in those settings.

- **Sort clothes by color:** "Let's put all the grays together, all the blues together, and all the whites together" helps your child's sensory development. Focus on one color at a time: "Let's get the red ones!"

- **Follow the Leader:** Giving your child directions like "Throw it in the trash" or "Put it by the door" helps her learn how to follow simple instructions.

- **Copycat (Housework Edition):** From two to three years old, children love to do what Mommy and Daddy are doing. Let them be present as you do housework. If they have a small broom or toy vacuum, they can follow along and copy what you do.

Age-Appropriate Chores: 3–4 Years

- **Switcharoo:** If your child has a sibling or friend, invite them to do a chore together like putting away toys in a storage bin. Each child brings you one toy at a time, and, taking turns, they put everything away.

- **Table time:** Letting your child follow you around the table helps him understand the concepts of *in*, *on*, and *under*. For example, "The fork goes on top of the napkin, and the water goes in the glass," or "If I put down the napkins, you have to put the forks on top."

- **Close what you open:** Reminding your child to "put the top back on once you're done" will let her practice opening and closing containers whenever she plays. Using small jars or storage containers for crayons, craft supplies, and small toys is a good way to keep organized and help your child work on sorting skills.

Age-Appropriate Chores: 4–5 Years

- **Getting ready:** Use a visual checklist to help your child get ready in the morning. The pictures will help your child develop self-care routines like putting on pajamas, going to the bathroom, brushing his teeth, and getting ready for bed. This will also help him start understanding time.
- **Cut your food:** At this age, your child can cut her own food. Take it a step further and let them pour, cut, and mash food. For example, your child could help you mash bananas for banana bread or potatoes for mashed potatoes.

Age-Appropriate Chores: 5–6 Years

- **Get a snack:** Your child can get his own snack from the fridge, get the correct silverware, eat, and clean up his snack on his own.
- **Daily tasks:** At this age, your child can be given more independent, but still supervised, chores. She is old enough to feed the dog or water the plants.

Age-Appropriate Chores: 6 Years and Up

- These chores will be independent and more sophisticated. In the kitchen, kids/teens can set the table, clear the table, and help Mom or Dad cook.
- **Some more heavy-lifting-type chores:** taking out the trash, light gardening, and doing laundry start to finish—washing, folding, and putting it away—will be perfect prep for college and beyond.

Expect Celebrations: Holiday (and Otherwise) Traditions

Now let's talk about those special occasions I mentioned. I love the way Oprah Winfrey states it: "The more you praise and celebrate your life, the more there is in life to celebrate." And one of the easiest ways to celebrate your life is to develop family routines, rituals, and traditions that you and your kids can expect and look forward to. Besides being fun and exciting, family traditions have a "potential protective role in fostering positive outcomes for children, adolescents, and emerging adults."[148] Developmental psychologists have theorized that routine and ritual "may contribute to the development of self-regulation . . . by providing concrete and predictable family relationship patterns."[149] As you work to develop traditions—holiday or otherwise—in your home, you will be gifting your children with predictability and stability that will serve them well into adulthood.

There are many different types of rituals and traditions you could establish. Chores, which we've already talked about, can be a kind of routine. But what about the family tradition of celebrations? And I mean those *big* celebrations: holiday parties and summer festivities, birthdays and graduations, career promotions and religious events—all these and more are celebrated by families everywhere, and they're important for a variety of reasons. Here are just a few of those reasons:

- Traditions bring meaning to our celebrations.
- Traditions help us bond with those we love.
- Traditions help enhance family values.
- Traditions help children feel secure.
- Traditions help connect extended families.
- Traditions provide a strong sense of identity.
- Traditions make us pause and be mindful.

That last one actually boosts your psychological well-being. According to social psychologist Fred Bryant and others, "when we stop to savor the good stuff, we buffer ourselves against the bad and build resilience."[150] According to researcher Hadassah Littman-Ovadia, "When we have something to look forward to, or look ahead to something worth celebrating, we feel more optimistic."[151] That something to look forward to could be starting a new job, starting a new school year, finishing a marathon, or celebrating a birthday.

Here are a couple of my family traditions. Even before we were parents, my husband and I loved having extended family gatherings in our home, a tradition we had adopted from my parents and largely took over responsibility for when my mother's Parkinson's began to progress. I wanted to bring our family together to celebrate the traditions my mom and dad had employed within our family. We've continued that tradition since.

For us, the last half of January is a *Birthday Extravaganza!* Jackson's birthday is on January 16, and Asher's is on January 20. They are blessed with many loving family members and friends who shower them with wonderful gifts. But with respect to tradition, I wanted my boys to know from a very early age that their birthdays are about more than just presents. We are also celebrating their existence!

There's an amazing tradition that was practiced in my children's Montessori preschool that I want to share with you. It's called a "Sun Celebration," and it refocuses kids on what their birthdays are all about.

"The Sun Celebration: The Birthday Walk around the Sun" is a ceremony that guides kids through a birthday walk for each year of their life. In preparation, the parents of the birthday child collect pictures of their child from the time around each previous birthday (including a newborn picture). On the day of the celebration, with the parents attending, the kids are arranged in a large circle, and an object that represents the sun is placed in the center. The parents of each child use the collected pictures to share a short life story about their child with the whole class. The birthday child then walks around the circle with a candle in hand while the children sing a special birthday song to the tune of "The Farmer in the Dell":

The earth goes around the sun,

The earth goes around the sun,

The earth goes around the sun,

and then _____ was one!
    (insert child's name)

This process is repeated for each year of life: the parents tell a story about the next year, then the child "walks around the sun" while the onlookers sing the song again, updating the last line with the next year of age. This "Sun Celebration" can also be experienced in your home, year after year. I did it for as long as my boys were interested!

Besides the big events like birthdays and holidays, research shows lots of benefits from small celebratory traditions as well, such as a special sleepover with Grandma and Grandpa or a special picnic with a friend. You name it, you can celebrate it! The increase in positive emotions from even these mini celebrations will make life easier to handle.[152] And if you choose the right moments, you can also teach your beautiful children how to celebrate themselves, not to produce a self-centered person, but rather a self-loving, joyful one.

We've talked about imparting self-love to your child. You can remind your child on a regular basis that life is full and that celebration of self is highly recommended. Teach your child to celebrate her accomplishments. I don't necessarily mean straight As or winning a math competition. Yes, of course, celebrate those amazing achievements, along with all the hard work involved, but also celebrate making new friends. Celebrate those mini achievements along the way to a larger goal, even if that goal is never ultimately achieved.

Teach your child to treat himself to something special, maybe candy, maybe a bubble bath with a favorite bath bomb, maybe just a special walk with a parent.

Most importantly, just teach your child to celebrate life! Every day is a new start. Every day is a celebration of being on this earth. I am writing this section on World Smile Day. How fitting. A smile is something to celebrate, don't you think?

Pro Parenting Tips: Celebrations

- Celebrate life every day! Just do it! Look for anything you can celebrate, no matter how small. Listen for birds chirping; celebrate their enthusiasm.
- Make celebrations a family tradition. Make this a core value of your family. Ask, "What should we celebrate this weekend?" TGIF!
- Expect that we all deserve to be celebrated. Teach your children to celebrate themselves. When a child does something kind, empathetic, or loving, notice it and say, "You should be really proud of yourself. Do you know what a wonderful person you are?"
- Get in the habit of loving to celebrate! Basically, see what you love in life and celebrate it. One of my boys likes to celebrate when he's done with his homework!

Pro Parenting Tips: EXTRA! Our Thankful Tree Tradition

Each November we use a Thankful Tree to take a step back and be consciously grateful and present as a family. Every day, each family member, including the parents, writes down on a card what he or she is grateful for. That person then hangs the card on the tree (real or imitation), and by Thanksgiving Day, the tree will be filled with words of thankfulness. It's a great way to celebrate all month long, not only on Thanksgiving, and it gets you into the habit of being thankful every day.

There are so many ways to incorporate a Thankful Tree into your home. It's great to incorporate age-appropriate art activities to get the kids into the spirit of being thankful! One year, I went to a craft store to pick up lighted twigs, leaves, and leaf-shaped cards to hang. When the boys were in preschool and loved finger painting, we made our tree from scratch and put it up on the wall. We also cut the leaves together to practice cutting. It wasn't exactly the most beautiful tree, but it was our tree.

Flexibility Is Your Friend: Managing Harmful Expectations

Now that we've talked about healthy expectations, let's talk about what happens when our expectations are inaccurate. It's impossible to list all the expectations that can potentially harm your child. Instead, I propose here a way of viewing your expectations that will help you make that determination between helpful and harmful yourself.

Children develop a sense of themselves from how they experience their relationship with their parents. Parental joy focuses on what brings the child joy and allows the child to focus on the joy inside of her. When there's a disconnect between what our children's interests, talents, and natural tendencies are and what we as parents expect or believe is best for them, children can feel that they are disappointing us in some way. This can inhibit a child's development of self-love and self-compassion and heighten feelings of shame and unworthiness.

Further, when a parent's expectations directly contradict how a child feels about himself—that is, the child feels he cannot be himself around his parents—he may feel forced to hide who he really is. The consequences of this scenario can range from minor to extremely serious.

For example, if a child with no interest in playing a musical instrument is expected to play that instrument and excel, the child will develop a sense of shame and disappointment. (Note here that exposure is different from forcing an expectation. All children should be exposed to music to see if there is an innate interest. But if you expose a child to something and there is no interest, allow the child to move on. Who knows? He may pick up the bug for music in a different way later on.)

Even more detrimental, however, is when a child is expected to be heterosexual or cisgender and is not. These children grow up with a deep sense of shame at the very core of their being. This shame then plays out in adulthood, and if it is not understood and professionally treated, it can pose a threat to the mental health and well-being of the individual.

If your child is hiding from you emotionally (or otherwise), your greatest help as a parent will be flexibility.

"Okay," you say, "but what does that look like?"

Think of a time when you were "in combat" with your kid. We've all been soldiers on that proverbial high-stress, high-volume battlefield. Kids (usually) strike first, then we strike back, and before you know it, we all end up in a foxhole. Now, as a parent, if you can cozy up to flexibility and make it your friend, you can remove yourself from that battlefield. Dr. Kate Roberts, a psychologist and parent coach, calls this ability "flexible responsiveness," or "a parent's ability to combine judgment and empathy to make the best parenting decision at any given time. The best parenting decision is always one that avoids a power struggle."[153] She says there are three signs that can alert parents to when flexible parenting is necessary and appropriate:

- Extenuating circumstances
- A child's difficulty managing typical stressors
- Parent fatigue and stress

Think about these three factors and how to use your flexibility as a superpower with your own children. In my house, Jackson needs *lots* of sleep. You know the nine to eleven hours recommended for elementary-school kids? Well, he's at eleven plus. There are some Mondays, after school and sports, when he literally has no more energy and goes straight to bed at around 6:30 or 7:00 p.m. At those times, I've learned that there's no need to insist on getting his homework done, eating dinner, or showering either. The kid just needs to sleep, and we let him. We just "go rogue."

The Science of Psychological Flexibility

The more you strive to be flexible in your parenting, the better your castle will be, and the better chances your children will have to fulfill their potential. Psychological flexibility is defined by researchers as the degree to which people can adapt to the demands of changing situations, shift their thinking patterns and perspectives, and balance the various needs and desires of their lives while maintaining consistent values. Research has also found that greater *general* psychological flexibility leads to greater *parenting* psychological flexibility, which results in more adaptive parenting practices and, in turn, decreased child behavior problems.[154]

Be flexible and malleable in your existing expectations, so that as your children grow and evolve into the best versions of themselves, you can step back and adjust when needed and truly allow them to be who they are meant to be. And be aware that adjusting your expectations may take more rethinking and learning than you might expect.

I experienced this process in the first class I taught as a kindergarten teacher. I was a young, first-time teacher, with thirty-three kids in my kindergarten classroom. Yes, I know it wasn't the perfect teacher-to-student ratio, but that's how it was. Now, before I ever walked into that classroom to teach those precious little five-year olds, I had been trained to know that routine is one of the most important tools in a teacher's toolbox. I knew I had been charged with getting these kindergarteners reading, prepping them for first-grade math, etc., but the pressure I put on myself as a new teacher to follow my initial expectations to a T was not realistic.

In theory, routine allows efficiency in teaching and creates security for students. That winning combo, along with engaging lessons and lots of social-emotional learning, can make for a fun-filled learning environment. A day can run more smoothly, and children are given the opportunity to deliver on teacher expectations.

Now let's talk reality. I can remember fondly the colorful schedule I posted for my students, right up at the front of the classroom, perfectly placed at eye level for each child. We referred to it daily, multiple times, to guide the kids through morning circle, reading, math, etc. And while our schedule worked beautifully most of the time, there were times I had to just toss up my hands, smile, and go rogue. That's when I quickly learned that *flexibility is my friend*. And I adjusted. When I saw kids who were not engaged or struggling to keep it together, we went outside to run and shake off some of the stress. Ten minutes of that turned everything around and got all of us refocused. If kids didn't feel comfortable yet reading aloud in class, they could call on a friend for help. Small tweaks were all it took. And guess what? We all survived, and my students thrived.

Now I know I said I went rogue, but being flexible doesn't mean losing control of the situation. In fact, flexibility is just as important as routine, even though every teacher believes in routine and has adapted, due to their education, to thinking of routine as a greater priority. In order to make the best decision for my students, the one that would actually help me achieve their learning goals, I had to adjust my expectations and my priorities.

So now let's bring this concept back to parenting. In parenting, flexibility is essential. Dr. Roberts places flexibility first in her "FAST" parenting model (flexibility, authority, structure, and transition), which is designed to help parents be more effective problem solvers in real time. The model also teaches parents how to manage parent-child interactions in a way that builds a stronger parent-child connection. Dr. Roberts says, "Flexible parenting encourages parents to use their discretion and judgment in daily decision making, while adhering to necessary structure and routine."[155]

Flexibility is your superpower. It allows you to be malleable and adaptable when crises, smaller changes, and just plain new information cross your path. Life is not a straight line. Flexibility frees you up to be the parent you want to be, a compassionate and empathetic one, rather than the parent you think you *must* be.

Accept that routines are meant to be broken. Routine is important in regular, everyday situations, but life is not "regular" all the time. Give yourself the grace to embrace flexibility. Expect to use it a lot. It doesn't mean you are failing. It means you are adjusting to the world and circumstances around you.

Teaching Flexibility—Anywhere, Anytime

In addition to learning flexibility yourself, let's not forget about teaching your kids how to be flexible. Show kids that flexibility and the ability to adapt is just part of life. There is security in knowing that there are ways to handle the inevitable bumps in the road.

Teach and model flexibility for kids. If kids witness your flexibility and know that circumstances matter, they too can adapt and move more freely in everyday situations. Talk about recognizing options and listening to others. Ask, "How can I help you get unstuck?" and then listen to the answer.

You can see flexibility, or lack thereof, on any playground at any time. One mother I talked to told me about her seven-year-old son who didn't want to share his brand-new basketball at the park because he didn't want it to get lost or stolen. He was unable to be flexible, which kept him from playing a basketball game with his friends, missing out on lots of potential fun.

Here's another example: A teacher friend of mine told me of a fifth-grade girl who, during a group assignment of building a robot, decided that her way was the only way and came up with what she thought was the perfect plan. While the other children were at lunch, she took apart the half-built robot. When they returned, she told them they had to do it her way. You can guess what happened next. The other kids went running to their teacher and the entire group was forced to start again. The children were not happy with the decision this young girl had made. This inflexibility caused chaos, more work, and lots of hurt feelings.

So how do you curb this rigidity when you spot it in your kids? It's a lot like curbing inflexibility in adults. Teaching our children to adapt and to consider others' feelings and ideas is one way to start. Teaching our children how flexibility can be their friend, by modeling it, also allows for this superpower to benefit them as well.

Here's another example you might be familiar with. Partway through 2020, Laura Wasser, known as "Hollywood's divorce attorney," joined me on my podcast, *Kids under Construction*, to talk about co-parenting during the pandemic.[156] Divorced or separated parents she had spoken with were panicked, concerned about whose household would be safest for the children they shared custody over. With what the "new normal" was presenting to them, how would they be able to remain consistent in school, chores, and tech time? (That last one was a big issue, even for parents with set technology-use rules.) All the work they had put toward maintaining routine and safety for their children was suddenly in danger of blowing up.

Laura Wasser told me she wanted parents to understand that they had power in flexibility. "Even without a global crisis," she said, "we generally try to recommend that parents try to adhere to the Three Cs—communication, consideration, and cooperation—and really, really listen to each other." Flexibility, done right, is the Three Cs in action.

In closing, here's a revised version of an article I wrote in May 2015.

Why I Said "Yes" to *Diary of a Wimpy Kid*, Even Though at First It Didn't Make Sense

It's not like I suggested it. He begged me. I mean, I told both my boys we needed to get their summer reading lists in order, but Jackson picked the title *Diary of a Wimpy Kid*. He said he really wanted to read the series and start with Book 1.

I told Jackson, who was six at the time, that I wasn't sure it was age appropriate (due to the words and situations). The book is really for eight- to twelve-year-olds, and there are a lot of mildly offensive words such as *jerk, stupid, dumb, dork, heck, shoot, freak,* and *butt.* Even milder expressions, like *stinky poo, screw loose,* and *suck it up,* are also right there in black and white.

Not quite sure what to do, I headed with him to the bookstore. The entire time I was thinking, *once he gets inside and starts shopping, he'll find something else.*

We arrive, and of course, the first thing he says to the young lady behind the desk is "Do you have *Diary of a Wimpy Kid?*"

Okay, now I must deal with it. He proudly follows the lady to the shelf, and she hands it to him. Once he's gripped it, a great big smile appears on his face. He tells me he's ready, he's got it, and let's go. (Likely trying to get me out of there before I could come up with another excuse not to get it. But I'm way ahead of him.)

I tell Jackson to sit down and read me the first page. I figure maybe it will be too tough to get through and that the comprehension might not be there. Not the case. The kid gets through the first page and is able to tell me what it all meant. I do have to help him with the word *specifically,* but that's it.

How do you say no to a kid who really, really, really wants to read something, even if he's a bit young for the content? I couldn't. I decided to talk to him about the use of what he calls "the S word" (*stupid*) and all the others, as those are not words he will be using. He agreed. He laughed and said he couldn't believe he was really reading words like *jerk* and *dumb*. It was as if he was getting away with something. For me, it was secretly the cutest thing ever.

Skip to us at home, me reading along with Jackson and explaining to him what "cooties" are and that they really aren't all that bad after all. Yeah, he's six, but he can handle it. Maybe in some ways, reading those "bad" words will become a way for him to better understand at a younger age how hurtful they are, guiding him to have a deeper sense of empathy.

What I really want you to take away from this chapter is that some expectations, the helpful ones, can be life changing, and that you truly can tune your mindset toward positivity. The harmful expectations are more of a distraction on your parenting path that will only pull you away from what you truly desire for your family. As you adjust and discard harmful expectations, don't forget that you can use your superpower, flexibility. Flexibility helps you go easy on yourself and your kids. Learn to make flexibility and positivity the default in your feelings and actions. Then, as you educate yourself and your children (the topic of the next chapter), and new information creates new rules, you will be prepared to change your expectations for the better.

Pro Parenting Tips: Building Flexibility into Everyday Parenting

These suggestions are from the *Beyond Discipline* series by the Positive Parenting Connection.[157]

- Involve children in making decisions when possible.
- Inventory current needs to decide based on the present moment.
- Don't get stuck on *musts* and *shoulds* if something is not working.
- Trust children to do things for themselves, even if it doesn't turn out perfectly or quite how you wished it would.
- Have routines to establish predictability—not to reward, punish, or control.
- Schedule in extra time whenever possible, so that special moments don't necessarily have to be lost or abandoned.
- Ask questions and welcome cooperation instead of making demands.
- Accept your child's feelings as authentic expression, not something you must control or squash.
- Dare to do things differently, be ridiculous, and cultivate laughter—this will help you relax and let go!
- Say yes when you can and say no with kindness.

Chapter 7:

Education

It is easier to build strong
children than to repair broken men.
—Frederick Douglass

I started teaching when I was in fifth grade. I'm serious! My little classroom was in my childhood home in our second den, downstairs, away
from all the noise usually present upstairs, what with four other siblings
engaged in their own activities. My students were two of my neighbors, sisters from just down the street (a great teacher-student ratio!).
Occasionally we would have others join us, but when we didn't, the two
sisters were happy to stick it out. For at least two long, hot summers, I
set up my little school room just so and filled a lesson plan book with
notes, ideas, and color coding. I think I taught every subject—except
for math, which figures, given that I'm a writer now. We also read
books, did lots of art projects, and talked about our lives and the places
we'd travel to around the world when we were all grown up.

I have always loved learning and teaching. I was that kid who didn't
mind summer coming to an end, who loved the new school year and
all that the back-to-school bustle entailed. It's part of who I am. But
my love of school is really a love of learning. Anything that I'm interested in, I'll dive in and try to learn it. And what I learn, I want to
teach, whether it be as the leader of my own fifth grade summer school
class of two, an elementary school teacher, a journalist on the news, a
journalism adjunct professor at UCLA Extension, a guest writer for
Harvard's Graduate School of Education's Making Caring Common

Project, a specialist on The Dr. Phil show, or anything in between—I love teaching, and I love learning.

For children, learning starts immediately, years before school teachers begin to share parents' educational responsibilities. Just as a teacher uses certain tools to set students up for success, parents can use these same tools in the home. Children thrive in this type of mindful learning environment. Benjamin Franklin says it best: "A house is not a home unless it contains food and fire for the mind as well as the body." You know the saying: "You are your child's first teacher." I take that literally, and I practice it in every way I know how. This book is what I have been putting into practice for twelve years now. I am transferring what I learned in the classroom as an elementary school teacher, as well as in my work as a parenting reporter, and putting it into practice in the home. The research I've collected for you here will help prepare you to start educating your children early and reap the scientifically proven benefits. You'll learn about useful tools to emphasize learning in the home and methods to stay involved when your child begins school.

To get us started on this enormous topic, here are some of my favorite quotes on education and learning:

- "Education is not the learning of facts, but the training of the mind to think." —Albert Einstein
- "Education is the most powerful weapon which you can use to change the world." —Nelson Mandela
- "Live as if you were to die tomorrow. Learn as if you were to live forever." —Mahatma Gandhi
- "If you are planning for a year, sow rice; if you are planning for a decade, plant trees; if you are planning for a lifetime, educate people." —Chinese Proverb
- "The function of education is to teach one to think intensively and to think critically. Intelligence plus character—that is the goal of true education." —Martin Luther King
- "I never did a day's work in my life. It was all fun." —Thomas Edison

- "It's not that I'm so smart. It's just that I stay with problems longer."
  —Albert Einstein

Raising a Learner for Life

The research is clear: Early education matters, and the earlier, the better. That's easier said than done. When I interviewed Dr. Kathleen Sweck about childhood reading, Dr. Sweck explained that children are not being read to as often as they should be. One of the major issues is what she called "time poverty," that in our very busy world and households (especially if both parents are working), finding the time to read, even for just thirty minutes a day, is difficult. Fortunately, if you're struggling to prioritize learning in your home, there are many tools available to you.

Case in point, one of my very first stories as a parenting reporter was a feature on the national organization Reach Out and Read.[158] Reach Out and Read provides books to pediatricians, who then pass them on to parents and model reading out loud to their children beginning from six months of age. This service reaches one in four low-income families, helping 4.7 million children annually. Here's what that looks like:

A mother of a two-year-old girl, Eliza, explained to me that she didn't prioritize reading to Eliza until Dr. Sweck offered her a book. She told me she didn't even think about making the time. But now she believes Reach Out and Read will make a difference in her daughter's life. And she's willing to make it a priority, which will bring her and Eliza many benefits. Reach Out and Read's statistics show that kids who have participated in the Reach Out and Read program start school with a six-month developmental advantage. And this amazing organization is only one example of the great benefits of early education in the home.

Let's step into the twenty-first century with Stanford researchers Ben York and Susanna Loeb, who founded a program called Ready4K.[159] This techy parenting tool gives parents fun facts and easy tips via text messages about how to maximize existing family routines and engage in more home learning activities. Yes, you too can get a quick lesson plan from Stanford researchers on how to teach your child at home. Just go to https://www.ready4k.parentpowered.com to get those helpful tips by text. Super cool!

See? Tools are out there for you; you just have to use them! But there are even more ways for you to make learning happen in the home.

Early Learning in the Home

Develop a mindful learning environment from the start by incorporating lessons into daily life. Get creative! For example, get your kids into the kitchen early. Have them read recipes out loud, help you measure and stir, and even create new family recipes. And don't worry about the mess! Even if those new recipes are a flop, it's all a part of learning.

Repeat activities and lessons often. Repetition helps learning happen, so try not to get frustrated—with your child or yourself. Little ones need repetition and reminders for the lesson to sink in. The awareness that repetition is part of parenting and teaching will ease any pressure you might feel.

Expose your child to everything you can, and I mean *everything*. Do whatever it takes to get out into the world and experience the world. Play every day, read every day, and do something fun as often as you can. Exposure to life is exhilarating and develops the brain.

Find people who get your kid. Remember when I talked about mentors in chapter 5? I am always on the hunt for people my children can bond with who will also give them opportunities to learn. I have found music teachers, chess teachers, and coaches, who see my kids and empathize with them. Their world is widened, they learn how to invest in their passions, and I get a break from being their only teacher.

Don't forget to incorporate social-emotional learning. Research shows that SEL, social-emotional learning, not only improves achievement by an average of eleven percentile points, but also increases prosocial behaviors (such as kindness, sharing, and empathy), improves student attitudes toward school, and reduces depression and stress among students.[160] You can help your child learn these skills by modeling them and by discussing them often in your home.

Help your child grow a love of learning. Researcher Ronald Williamson says, "When teachers have high expectations for students and provide tasks that are engaging and of high interest, students build self-esteem, increase confidence, and improve academic performance."[161] Use this information in your home. Set achievable expectations for your children and help them to engage in all types of learning. I love the way Maya Angelou expresses this idea,:"If you're always trying to be normal, you will never know how amazing you can be."

Don't be afraid to fail. Not everything you do will be a success. For example, I think I'm crafty, that I make fabulous craft items for the home, but when I see what other parents can put together . . . let's just say that my talents lie elsewhere. But I still do projects with my kids at home. They're never perfect, ever. But it's okay. There's learning in failing too.

Early Learning in Preschool

Now let's talk about preschool, when your child starts learning outside the home in earnest. Because of that, picking the perfect preschool *for your child* takes time and touring. I can remember friends and neighbors asking me, "How many more schools are you going to look at?" I probably looked at eight or ten preschools and participated in all their "Mommy and Me" classes before I chose. My children's needs won't match up precisely with yours, but here are some useful guidelines I discovered:

As you already know from chapter 2, I am a huge fan of the Montessori Method. Maria Montessori (1870–1952) was an Italian physician and educator best known for the philosophy of education that bears her name. Many of Montessori's sayings about education have resonated in my life, but here are a few:

- "The greatest sign of success for a teacher . . . is to be able to say, 'The children are now working as if I didn't exist.'"[162]
- "Joy, feeling one's own value, being appreciated and loved by others, [and] feeling useful and capable of production are all of enormous value for the human soul."[163]
- "Never help a child at a task at which he feels he can succeed."[164]

You may see a pattern in these quotes, and you'd be right! Teaching children to do things for themselves is one of the most central principles to the Montessori Method. As such, the Montessori Method uses a technique called "job work" to help children achieve autonomy. Some jobs are individual while others are performed with partners. Some of the jobs for preschool children include pouring water from a small pitcher into a cup, counting beans, or buckling buckles. These activities teach self-reliance, build confidence, and encourage working with others. I love it all!

Of course, while counting beans can be fun and playful, it's also academic and usually teacher directed. What about free play, the time when kids can climb trees, play pretend, and just run around? Free play allows for creativity and adventure in learning as well as teaching resiliency, confidence, and social skills, making it just as important as academic learning, if not more so, for a child's developing brain.[165] But you don't have to choose between free play and academics.

When I finally chose my perfect preschool for my kids, I picked one that was Montessori-based with an infusion of directed play and free play. That way, my kids got to have both! The school also put on spectacular shows during the winter and spring. One of the parents was a Hollywood set designer, and we had a wonderful teacher's assistant who sewed the most beautiful costumes. Asher as the Chameleon King and Jackson as a little Frenchman are some of the most brilliant memories I have of that time.

My point is that I found a place that exposed them to all sorts of learning by blending a variety of methods. I do not subscribe to one method over the other. Learning is everywhere and in everything. There are many mixes out there, so have confidence that you can find the combination that works best for your children.

Most importantly, you must find a place with loving and caring teachers. You want the people around your child to know and see your child. To do that, you have to tour, research, and talk to other parents about their experiences. Tell the teachers about your child. Help them understand who he is, and then communicate with them regularly throughout your child's time there. Your role is crucial. You are his voice until he learns how to use his own.

Pro Parenting Tips: Picking the Perfect Preschool

- Research thoroughly and ahead of time:
  - » Start a year in advance
  - » Tour
  - » Participate in lots of "Mommy and Me" classes, which will acclimate your child to the environment and let you observe her to see whether it's a good fit
  - » Attend preschool fairs
  - » Talk to other parents
- Understand the philosophy of the school:
  - » Is the preschool play-based, academic-based, or a combo?
  - » What is the philosophy of discipline? Is it in line with your discipline at home?
  - » Is the school's curriculum in line with current educational research?
- Learning the ABCs and 123s:
  - » Is the school incorporating the building blocks for kindergarten readiness?

> » Are kids learning their ABCs and 123s through stories, singing, and games?
> » Are ABCs and 123s displayed for children to see?
> - Play time:
>   » Research indicates that children learn via play. Is play part of the curriculum?
>   » Do the teachers and other parents encourage an atmosphere of play?
>   » How do the teachers interact with the children? Are they asking the children questions? Are they engaging the children? Are they loving?
>   » Is your child happy, safe, and learning?
> - Trust your gut: Only you, the parent, knows what's best for your child.

Staying Involved in Your Child's Schooling

So you've chosen a great preschool (or elementary, middle, or high school) for your child. Congratulations! That's a big step. However, don't fall into the trap of letting your child's school do all the work. It's vital to still be an active participant in your child's education once it's shifted outside the home. That can be tricky, especially if your children aren't interested in sharing, but there are a variety of methods to get your kids talking and make learning a family activity.

Fifteen Ways to Ask Your Child, "What Did You Do at School Today?"

My advice comes to you after years of interviewing kids as a journalist and understanding that they are the toughest interviewees ever! When I pick Jackson and Asher up from school, I want to hear it all. I want to hear about every single part of their day. Heck, if I could, I'd be a fly on the wall. But I can't, so it's up to them to tell me what the day entailed and it's up to me to get it out of them. They're not going to tell me *everything* I want to know, but there are a few ways to get an answer to the question, "What did you do at school today?" and hear more than "I don't know."

What's helped me and what can help you is to interview your kid (not to the point of exhaustion), but just enough to get some good "intel." *Always* ask open-ended questions. If you ask simple "yes" or "no" questions, that's exactly what you'll get. Instead, make a game out of it! Then sneak in a few questions that will ensure some juicy details:

1. Who makes you laugh the most at school?
2. What was your teacher wearing?
3. What was the first thing you did in school?
4. What was the last thing you did in school?
5. What did you see in another kid's lunch box that you'd like for your lunch?
6. What is your favorite part of the classroom and why?
7. What game did you play during recess?
8. What part of the day did you like the least and why?
9. Tell me how you felt when you first walked into the classroom. Nervous, excited?
10. What was one thing your teacher said to you that was silly?
11. Guess how old your teachers are.
12. Give me three chances to figure out what your favorite subject is. And if I don't get it, you can have ten extra minutes before bedtime.
13. What color uniform (or outfit) are you planning on wearing to school tomorrow?
14. If you could go back to school today and start the day over, what would you do differently and why?
15. What are you looking forward to tomorrow at school?

Acing Your Parent-Teacher Conference

You already know that before I became a reporter, I was a teacher. I was often surprised at how quiet the parents were during our time together. I felt that I wanted more information about the kids I was teaching. I also wanted a stronger connection with the parents.

Now, as a parent myself, I know how important my role is in nurturing this very important relationship. We all must work together to ensure success: mom/dad, child, and teacher. We are a team.

Our children spend most of their day with their teachers. Your child's teacher is there to ensure your child's academic success. So when parent-teacher conferences roll around, you want to be there. It's that precious time to get the one-on-one attention you and your child deserve. You want to get to know your kid's teacher and you want your kid's teacher to understand your kid. Help your child connect with his teacher to ensure not only a successful academic school year but a happy one!

Here's a guide and some things to remember to ace your parent-teacher conference:

- Help your child advocate for herself. Before the conference, ask your child what's on her mind regarding school. This is a great time to take the opportunity to advocate for your child. Ask your child what she needs. Is there something that she would like to change or try at school? Is there something the teacher and you as a parent can do to help?

- Show up! Don't miss your parent-teacher conference unless there is an emergency. That means both parents. This will allow you to understand exactly what the teacher is expressing. It's also beneficial to be able to bounce ideas off one another. This is one of your most important meetings as parents!

- Go in with an open mind. There is no room for preconceived notions or engaging in rumors. What one parent/child may have experienced with your teacher may not reflect the majority of children's experiences. You and your child have a unique relationship with the teacher, so rely on your own experience rather than others'.

- Really listen to what the teacher is expressing about your child, even if it conflicts with your experience at home. Are you the same at home as you are out in the world? Likely, the answer is no. So, ask questions and then pay attention.

- Get on the same page as your child's teacher. Remember, your child's teacher is the person caring for and working to ensure your child's academic success. Do your best to enhance what the teacher is trying to accomplish rather than obstructing it.

- Tell the teacher about your kid. Let the teacher know what your child is like on the sports field, during downtime, or who his friends are. Knowing what makes your kid tick will help the teacher craft the ideal classroom experience for him.

- Don't be afraid to ask questions. If your child needs extra help or the teacher wants her to focus on something, ask specifically what you should do at home to help your child transfer that to the classroom. Ask the teacher to spell it out. It's okay. Take the time now so that none of you have to play catch-up later.

- Remember, your child's teacher is only human. Teachers make mistakes too. Be empathetic and realize that in most cases your child's teachers are doing their best. If you're empathetic, the teacher is also more likely to want to understand and be empathetic toward your child.

Monthly Family Meetings

Another way to get involved in your child's education is to have monthly family meetings, something I am a big believer in. Family meetings teach children so many valuable social and life skills: listening, brainstorming, problem solving, mutual respect, cooperation, and concern for others. They also give parents opportunities to avoid power struggles, respectfully share control, avoid micromanaging children, and listen in a way that invites sharing. They can even become a heartfelt and cherished family tradition.

Frequent meetings are a message to kids that parents cherish what matters to them and what they are expressing. And when kids are trying to figure out what makes themselves tick, a family meeting provides a safe space for self-evaluation and discovery. Family meetings also provide structure, taking a family away from the chaos of life to refocus on what matters to them.

With those goals in mind, don't be overwhelmed. Family meetings don't have to be formal, and they shouldn't be long or drawn-out. Be flexible on time. For younger kids, anywhere from ten to twenty minutes is perfect, though older children may need more. To help maintain order, have the person who is speaking hold a special rock or trinket to indicate he or she has the floor. (In the early days of our family meetings, a Lego Batman served this purpose.) This will help maintain the feel of a meeting and really develop those listening skills, not only for kids, but for parents too.

Here's a model agenda for your first family meeting:

1. Start out with compliments: Mention improvements being made in the home, compliment kindness shown, and share what you are grateful for.
2. Bring up concerns.
3. Discuss solutions to problems and talk about progress already made.
4. Talk about the upcoming calendar, what is coming up next in school, family functions, etc.
5. Conclude with a game, prayer, or meditation.

Educational Family Activities: Learning in Chess

A family meeting is formal, but any spur-of-the-moment activity can be a learning experience for all concerned. That means you too. In fact, you might be surprised what your kids have to teach you. To illustrate that point, let me tell you about my family's tradition of playing chess together.

Before my kids got me into it, I had never played a game of chess in my life. (I was more of a checkers kid.) It took seven-year-old Asher and eight-year-old Jackson to get me to finally try it out. They argued that it's anyone's game. Well, not in my experience. I've been playing chess for a couple of years now, and they still dominate me, but one day I *will* prevail! I learn something new every match. It's the ultimate brain game. Did you know that after each person makes one move, there are four hundred different possible positions? Try wrapping your head around this now: after three moves each, there are over *nine million* different possible positions.[166]

My boys got into chess thanks to Mr. Robert Romano—or, as I like to call him, just Romano. He's one of those teachers who make you feel like the most special kid in the world. And so, when Romano urged my boys to learn to play chess, they jumped at the idea.

First the boys started playing, then their friends started playing, and after a while we went to their very first chess tournament, which was an interesting experience because parents aren't even allowed to watch. That's right! You bring them there—and you can help them find their boards and opponents, somewhere in this giant room lined with tables upon tables and chess boards set up side by side—but then there's a countdown to get the parents out: "Ten, nine, eight"—the kids start yelling, "Out!" to their parents—"seven, six, five"—"Stop taking pictures!"—"three, two, one. Parents out, and let the games begin!"

The first time in the waiting area is agonizing. It's the same kind of setup as a soccer game: everyone brings their fold-up chairs and coolers filled with drinks and snacks, but you don't see any of the action. You are stuck waiting for your kid to walk through those double doors with an announcement. Sometimes it's a thumbs-up, sometimes it's a thumbs-down, sometimes there's crying, and other times it's just pure elation. Yes, chess is a roller coaster of emotions, and parents are along for the ride, but you're basically stuck in the trunk, in the dark, until the ride is over . . . then you get to deal with the aftermath.

Chess players are assigned opponents based on their rating, which moves up or down based on their win rate in the last few matches. So, when Asher had a few solid tournament showings, he jumped up to a rating where he was stuck playing against middle and high school kids. The next tournament didn't go that well. In fact, when it looked like things couldn't get any worse, they did.

It was Asher's fourth match of the day. He and I found his opponent being coached by his dad in Mandarin while moving the pieces on the board at what looked like eighty miles an hour. And here we were, a mom with no insight to give, no second language, and Asher not looking very confident. All I could do was give him a kiss on his cheek and say, "Have fun!" That's chess.

Now this story doesn't have a twist at the end, with a come-from-behind win. In fact, in less than ten minutes, Asher was out, thumbs down, and looking for a private hug away from all the other parents anxiously awaiting their kids' entrance into the waiting room.

Losing is no fun. Asher huddled in my arms, beaten down and exhausted. But then Romano made his way to us with clipboard in hand, pencil behind ear, and a sweet smile.

"Asher," he said, "how did it go?" (He already knew how it went.)

Asher said, "I lost."

Romano sighed, sat down beside us, and said, "You didn't lose. You *learned.*"

I was as surprised as Asher. We both looked at Romano—this chess teacher, pal, and all-around, great human being—and perked up.

Then Romano said, "So tell me what happened," and Asher responded (in another language as far as I was concerned. I just can't keep up when they talk chess without a board for a visual).

Romano listened and again said, "So you learned?"

Asher picked up his head, smiled his biggest smile of the day, and said, "Yeah, I guess I learned."

Success, success, success.

This lesson was not only for Asher, but for me and now his dad and Jackson as well. For us, the outcome of every chess match, every sports game, every anything that has to do with winning or losing is now not about losing anymore. It's about *learning*. What a gift to be able to use in the world! Of course, as my boys grow, and winning starts to really mean winning and losing starts to really mean losing (such as in poor grades, competitive sports, and job searches), they can still learn something from that—most of all understanding that winning isn't everything, and learning is.

In our home, chess also plays another very important role. It gives my two grade-school boys the upper hand with me (as they like to call it). They are so much more knowledgeable than I am on this topic. That doesn't happen every day, and it allows them to teach me something. It's pure, and it's real. It gives us another way to bond, it gives them confidence, and it teaches me that I am always learning and, most importantly, learning from them. Chess really taught us all to think about learning as an ongoing, always-present piece of the puzzle of life. You can always learn more in chess. You can always get better. The possibilities are limitless. My hope is that we can all play chess together for many years to come. It's our newest family tradition. And maybe it can become yours too!

When you're considering what learning activities to incorporate into your family, knowing the benefits is key. It's no secret that there are so many brain benefits to chess. Chess builds problem-solving abilities; improves children's cognition, verbal skills, and critical thinking; exercises both sides of the brain; builds confidence; improves test scores—the list goes on and on. Asher's chess teacher tells me chess helps Asher "slow down." Asher is fast at everything he does, so learning how to slow down and think through options is a huge benefit for him. For Jackson, who is methodical in his thinking, chess reinforces his strengths.

So how can you become fearless and just give chess a try? One, get a kid or an adult to show you how each piece moves. Be patient with yourself; it takes time to take it all in. Once you know the bare minimum, just start playing matches whenever you can. Challenge anyone: man, woman, or child. In our family we occasionally do mini-chess tournaments in the evenings. My husband and I usually each play against one kid, then we move onto the semifinals. Sometimes we don't even stop for dinner.

If you believe that you and your children are always learning and growing, your families can thrive. Take the idea that Romano shared with Asher, and the well-known quote from John C. Maxwell, "Sometimes you win and sometimes you learn," and let it open your minds and provide you with new perspectives. Here are some more quotes I love about learning that might inspire you:

- "I am still learning." —Michelangelo, at age eighty-seven
- "The more that you read, the more things you will know. The more that you learn, the more places you'll go." —Dr. Seuss
- "Tell me and I forget. Teach me and I may remember. Involve me and I learn." —Benjamin Franklin

Pro Parenting Tips: Making Games a Positive Learning Experience

- Find ways that your kid can teach you. Make it legitimate and give them the space to teach you in the way that makes sense to them. Give them the ability to learn how to be a teacher.
- Change the way that you talk about winning and losing. Make it a mantra in your home: "I didn't lose. I learned." Follow it up with a question: "What did you learn?" Winning is fine, but it's not the most important thing to take away from any competitive action. Losing is *learning*. Maintaining this perspective really allows kids to grow.

- The benefits of chess are endless. It improves math skills, goal setting, planning and consequences, and so much more. If chess isn't something your family enjoys, look for other activities with similar benefits.
- Call out compassion! When someone shows compassion to you or your child, be grateful for that compassion. Praise that act! Just as Romano showed compassion to Asher after his chess match, really see the compassion and let your child know what it looks like and sounds like.
- Accept where you and your children are in the learning process. Know you are growing. Watch your learning curve expand. As Walt Whitman said, "Be curious, not judgmental."
- Remember, learning is everywhere! Learn from your family members. Learn from your children. Provide an environment where learning is celebrated!

Homework Hassles . . . HA!

And now let's talk about the part of learning in the home that has been a cause of so much stress and concern for so many families: homework.

The homework debate has been ongoing for decades, at sporting events, at birthday parties—anywhere parents gather, homework is always a topic of conversation, and it's usually not positive. The laundry list of complaints is a long one:

"My kid is staying up all hours of the night to do her homework."

"I can't help my kid do his homework."

"The homework my kids are getting is useless."

And so on. Basically, homework isn't fun for *anyone*, parents included.

Okay, that's a little unfair. There is some fun on occasion. I remember one of Jackson's third-grade assignments, for which he was asked to prepare a breakfast menu, with pricing, etc., for his math class (it was the money unit). He was so excited about this assignment that he ended up making one of the items on his menu for me and my husband to eat.

Sadly, for many parents and children, this sort of enjoyment is rare. Figuring out how to get kids to do their homework without a hassle is probably one of the biggest hurdles for parents of school-age children. I've seen it on both sides, as a parent and as a former teacher.

Here's a Facebook post that relates the struggle of one such mom (who will remain anonymous):

> I eventually gave up. My son was a perfectionist. He would ask, and I would guide, but he hated it because he always thought I knew the answer and wouldn't tell him. Sometimes I would, sometimes I wouldn't, but I wanted him to learn how to find the answers. I had been told to let him unwind after school, be super organized (label folders, have a non-disruptive workspace—not the kitchen table), lots of tools to do the work, pens, pencils, crayons, etc. Work for 20 minutes and then take a break. Use the break as a reward to keep him motivated to keep working. Tell a story that related to him to help him understand the concept. I finally gave up because we argued way too much about it. I gave him resources for help. Homework help line, friends, the internet, mentors, teachers, staying after school, and I also offered a tutor. I am happy to say he is in his 3rd semester of college and is killing it. He is working 25-plus hours a week and getting As and Bs. He is a great college student. I firmly believe in not doing the work for the child. I have seen lots of assignments that a child probably didn't even touch: don't do that. Let your child fail. The school-aged

years are when they should experience failures where the consequences aren't life altering and they can learn to pick themselves up, dust themselves off and do better.[167]

Can you relate? What a whirlwind of emotions, trials, and tribulations. But did you notice that in the end all was okay? Take that hard-learned lesson and remember it when homework gets tough.

Now let's add a little perspective. When I was a teacher, I always believed in the concept of homework, that it taught responsibility and practiced what a child learned in school, as long as it was used in a meaningful way.

As a parent, I've realized that too much homework can be detrimental not only to the child individually (restricting the ability to nurture other interests) but to family life. There is now some very important research indicating that in some contexts and age groups, homework is not helpful to students. If you incorporate this belief and hard evidence into your family life, you can begin to work toward a more peaceful homework mindset—a life-altering experience.

Strategies for Effective Homework

In August 2016, I interviewed the co-founder of Stanford's program Challenge Success, Dr. Denise Pope, about the research on homework. I was fascinated by what I was hearing and ecstatic, to say the least, upon learning about the research.

According to her, here's what parents need to know:

- Kindergarten through fourth grade: Homework does not correlate to academic success.
- Middle to high school: Homework is useful when used appropriately, but children should spend no more than ninety minutes to two hours on it. Beyond that amount, there is no correlation with academic performance and success.
- Homework should be meaningful, as when, for example, a teacher assigns reading one chapter in *To Kill a Mockingbird* in preparation for the next day's class discussion.

- Individualized homework plans can help bridge the gap between standardized curriculums and personal need.

An article summarizing Stanford's findings on the elements of effective homework from August 2020 says the following:

> Given that much of the research points to little or no benefits of homework, we urge educators to take a hard look at their current practices and policies. Some educators in the lower grades might consider eliminating homework altogether, and just ask students to spend time reading for pleasure (which is positively connected to achievement) or allow them the extra time to enjoy time for play and time with family. At the very least, we suggest that educators and parents note the overwhelmingly positive research on the value of engaging students in learning and the ties between student engagement and achievement in school. If homework is going to be assigned, it should be developmentally appropriate, meaningful, and engaging for the students.[168]

Be encouraged that schools are starting to take this research seriously. Malibu High School has a "Homework Policy" page on their website that includes guidelines and tips for parents, students, and teachers.[169] Here are a few of their parent tips:

- Act as cheerleaders and supporters, not homework police: Ideally, the child should be able to do the homework alone, without help from parents. Instead of checking, editing, or doing the work for the student, parents should provide necessary supplies and show an active interest in the content the student is learning.
- Work with your child to determine a healthy schedule of activities that will allow time to complete homework, work on projects, and study for tests—while still getting adequate sleep and time for play, family time and downtime.
- Teach techniques that can help children allocate their time wisely,

meet their deadlines, and develop good personal study habits.

- Encourage your children to self-advocate by working directly with their teachers if issues arise.

- Encourage teachers to work with both you and your student to create effective homework policies. Start by communicating with your own child's teacher about issues or homework challenges your child is facing.

- Recognize that a missed or poorly done homework assignment every now and then is not going to hurt your child in the long run. Parents can help students organize their time or prioritize assignments, but when parents regularly deliver forgotten assignments to school or step in to rescue a child at the last minute, they may be denying the child the opportunity to develop resilience.

Following this advice can drastically reduce the amount of stress children experience while doing homework. The Great Neck Public Schools has a document specifically on that topic, which says, in part, "Recognize that children learn in different ways and have different work styles—some do homework all at once, while others need to take frequent breaks. Discuss with your child the working conditions that will lead to the best homework outcomes."[170] For example, some kids prefer to sit in quiet spaces, and some may do better with music playing in the background.

I hope these resources encourage and help you. If your children's schools haven't yet begun these sorts of changes, consider becoming an advocate for healthier homework policies in your community.

Destressing the Daily Homework Routine

For now, kids are still getting homework, and lots of it, so what can you do? How do you incorporate this research into your child's daily homework routine? Here's what I do for my elementary-school boys:

- Tell your kids about the research. Why? It helps to ease the pressure. This gives kids the ability to not take it so incredibly seriously.

Remember the mom who described her son as a perfectionist? It doesn't have to be so intense. Of course, you want your child to always try his best, but ease up. If it helps, blame it on the research!

- Give your child the ability to take a break at home before moving into the homework mode. Try to remember that she's been in school all day, then maybe at an extracurricular activity, and after all that, there's still homework. I know a lot of parents just want to get it done so they don't have to deal with it or think about it. *I get it.* But when you get home from a busy day at work, do you want to get home and start working again? Likely the answer is no. Apply this same logic to your child.

- Don't compare your child to anyone else. Every child is unique, and every child will grow and develop at his own academic speed.

- Have compassion for your child when it comes to the homework load. Put yourself in her position. Let her know you're on her side.

- Help your child learn to trust himself as he works independently on homework. Don't hover. Let him learn that he can manage this aspect of school.

- Let your child know that school is her job. Expect that your child will do her work and maintain her best effort.

- Communicate with your child's teacher when homework is too hard or when homework is not finished. There is no need for any additional stress in relation to homework. If your child needs an extra day to complete an assignment, ask the teacher. If your child does not understand the assignment, ask the teacher for guidance. *Ask questions.* As your child gets older, help your child communicate with his teacher on his own. Self-advocacy is a necessary skill, and as soon as a child feels he can talk to his teacher without you, he'll be better for it.

Pro Parenting Tips: Speed Homework

If the boys have a packed after-school schedule on a particular day, I announce that we are doing "Speed Homework." The title sounds a little wacky, but this is a technique I came up with and started using a few years ago after I interviewed Denise Pope. It's simple, and it makes homework a game. (Remember the research!) My boys love it because they are so competitive. The basic principle is that we sit down together and focus for twenty to thirty minutes. No talking, no distractions. It's like a test. And it usually works. Of course, some days, they need more time, but this strategy gets them focused (an important skill across all aspects of life), it doesn't drag it out, they move past questions they do not understand, they don't take it so seriously—but seriously enough—and so on. Now . . . on your mark, get set, GO!

Raise Your Hand If You're a Lifelong Learner!

As I conclude this final chapter of *The C.A.S.T.L.E. Method*, I want you to know that this building block of your castle is not only about educating your children in the various parts of their lives, but also about having you, the parent, understand that this journey of parenthood is a lifelong learning process. It's how we feed that curiosity, the curiosity that we all feel, about how to best understand, support, and nurture our children as they become the best versions of themselves. If we stop learning as parents, we won't be able to meet our kids where they are, at a moment's notice, when they need us to help them grow.

In her book *Mindset: The New Psychology of Success*, Dr. Carol Dweck explains her finding that we all have different beliefs about the underlying nature of ability, especially with respect to learning and intelligence. To describe these beliefs, she coined the terms "fixed mindset" and "growth mindset." She found that children (and adults!) with a growth mindset believe that intelligence and abilities can be developed through effort, persistence, trying different strategies and learning from mistakes. "As you begin to understand the fixed and growth mindsets," she says, "you will see exactly how one thing leads to another—how a belief that your qualities are carved in stone leads to a host of thoughts and actions, and how a belief that your qualities can be cultivated leads to a host of different thoughts and actions, taking you down an entirely different road."[171]

I want you to begin thinking about yourself as a person with a growth mindset, as a lifelong learner in the parenting realm. I'm sure you're always learning and growing in other facets of your life; that's part of being human. But really focusing on lifelong learning as a parent will allow you a freedom you may have not ever experienced before. It's what I talked about in the introduction of this book. I told you I don't feel *perfect* in my parenting journey, but I do mostly feel satisfied with all I am doing. I want that for you too.

As I write this final chapter today, after years of working on this book, my two boys now are in middle school. All I have learned and practiced up to this point has provided a solid foundation for my boys and for my family, but as a lifelong learner, I know there's still a lot in front of me. Soon I'll have to get in tune in a new way and start seeing my boys as they grow into, and then out of, their teenage years. I will have to adjust based on how I see them unfold, expand, and mature as they make their way in the world. In short, I have to learn to see my boys as the people they are becoming, not what they have been.

I am excited, but I also feel a bit like I did when they were babies. Remember when I talked about not feeling very confident in my parenting journey early on? While those feelings have eased significantly as I've learned to manage my emotions and educate myself, I still worry. I am human.

I will continue to use the foundational building blocks in the CASTLE Method. They are truly what guide me. I will go back to trust and know that my husband and I, as parents—we've got this, and so do Asher and Jackson. They've got this. I can still guide and support them, but I must watch them fully develop a trust in themselves in order to fulfill their life dreams. Do you recall when I told you to be easy on yourself, as this is the very first time you are creating a family? Well, as you move from milestone to milestone in your kids' lives, remember that it's your first time for each milestone, again, and again, and again. Just be gentle with yourself. You have the tools you need; you know how to figure things out, and (one last reminder from me) when you parent, you know to start with compassion and end with compassion. You've got this!

Conclusion

Go confidently in the direction of your dreams.
Live the life you have imagined.
—Henry David Thoreau

Dear Reader,

First, I want to say thank you, thank you for listening to my message, taking it to heart, and growing and learning along with me.

As an aspiring author, I loved daydreaming about titles. It was fun, but many of them didn't quite encompass my message. There were three that had the most potential. The first title was *The Practiced Parent*, next up was *Kids under Construction* (which is also the title of my podcast and TV segment), and finally, there was *The C.A.S.T.L.E. Method*. As I wrote, I got really busy with life—being a mom, wife, daughter, sister, friend, and TV journalist. Finally, I put the book away, believing I would never truly become a published author. To borrow Dr. Dweck's wording, that was a fixed mindset. I now see those three titles as corresponding to the stages of how I evolved—and continue to evolve—as a parent.

The "practiced parent" was someone who was trying her best, mindfully parenting and educating herself to the best of her ability.

Kids under Construction came from a deep feeling of really wanting to know my children and to help other parents really know their own children too. As I've said, you are the person who knows your kid best—you, not any doctor, any expert in the field, no one. But if you can see your children through the lens of them evolving each day, each hour, and each minute, you will surely be able to parent them in compassion, acceptance, security, trust, love, expectations, and education. And you *will* figure out what is best for you, your child, and your family.

But being flexible and listening to others' opinions, research, and expertise are essential skills. Use the people who have the knowledge that you need. And so now you see where I'm going with this. *The C.A.S.T.L.E. Method* is the final title, and it's the one that stuck. I truly want you to take what you learn in this book, practice it as a parent, and really see who your kid is, so that you can build your family's dream castle.

Be compassionate to yourself. Find out what really makes you *you*. Grab a piece of it and show it to yourself and your kids. They'll love it. Use compassion with your kids more and more each day. It builds and builds until it's the first way you look at your child. And when you inevitably don't do so, forgive yourself.

Accept your child. I implore you. We know how damaging it is to not accept them. None of us is perfect, and we should let our kids in on that fact, so that they will be able to better embrace their own imperfections.

Provide emotional security for your children. Really let them share all of their emotions, even, and especially, when it is uncomfortable for you. Model managing your own emotions.

Trust your children and know they are capable. They need to master this skill, trusting themselves, to move through life, without needing any approval from you or anyone else on the planet. They are worthy.

Love your children. You know what to do there.

Expect the best for each and every single one of your family members. Please stay positive but leave space for all feelings. Expect joy, and if it doesn't come, tell yourself, "Dear Me, I've got this."

Finally, as long as you are a lifelong learner in what I believe to be the most important job in the world, you are good. You are open to new knowledge and evolving along with your child. You don't have to stay stuck in the place you are now. Always remember you have the power to build the CASTLE of your dreams as soon as you are ready to make the dream your reality.

Warmly,

Donna Tetreault

Endnotes

1. Heather S. Lonczak, "20 Reasons Why Compassion Is So Important in Psychology," Positive Psychology, September 13, 2021, https://positivepsychology.com/why-is-compassion-important/.

2. Ibid.

3. *Child Maltreatment 2019*, U.S. Department of Health & Human Services, Administration for Children and Families, Administration on Children, Youth, and Families, https://www.acf.hhs.gov/sites/default/files/documents/cb/cm2019.pdf.

4. Paul Gilbert, "The Origins and Nature of Compassion Focused Therapy," *British Journal of Clinical Psychology* 53 (2014): 19.

5. James N. Kirby, "Nurturing Family Environments for Children: Compassion-Focused Parenting as a Form of Parenting Intervention," *Education Sciences* 10, no. 3 (2020): 5, https://doi.org/10.3390/educsci10010003.

6. Joshua Schultz, "5 Differences between Mindfulness and Meditation," Positive Psychology, December 11, 2020, https://positivepsychology.com/differences-between-mindfulness-meditation/.

7. Deborah Bloom, "Instead of Detention, These Students Get Meditation," CNN Health, November 8, 2016, https://www.cnn.com/2016/11/04/health/meditation-in-schools-baltimore/index.html.

8. "Research," UCLA Mindful Awareness Research Center, accessed November 12, 2021, https://www.uclahealth.org/marc/research.

9. Ying Chen and Tyler J. VanderWeele, "Associations of Religious Upbringing with Subsequent Health and Well-Being from Adolescence to Young Adulthood: An Outcome-Wide Analysis," *American Journal of Epidemiology* 187, no. 11 (2018): 2355–64, https://doi.org/10.1093/aje/kwy142.

10. Ibid.

11. Chris Sweeney, "Religious Upbringing Linked to Better Health and Well-Being during Early Adulthood," Harvard T. H. Chan School of Public Health, News, September 13, 2018, https://www.hsph.harvard.edu/news/press-releases/religious-upbringing-adult-health/.
12. Donna Tetreault, "Dr. Judy Ho: Middle School and Mindfulness," February 22, 2021, in *Kids under Construction*, ABC4, podcast, episode 5, 42:29, https://www.iheart.com/podcast/269-kids-under-construction-60726054/episode/dr-judy-ho-middle-school-and-60728262/.
13. Ibid.
14. Mark Bertin, "A Daily Mindful Walking Practice," Mindful: Healthy Mind, Healthy Life, July 17, 2017, https://www.mindful.org/daily-mindful-walking-practice.
15. Ibid.
16. Martin Seligman, quoted in Kori D. Miller, "14 Health Benefits of Practicing Gratitude According to Science," Positive Psychology, September 10, 2021, https://positivepsychology.com/benefits-of-gratitude/.
17. Kathy Gottberg, "My Top 10 Favorite Quotes from Abraham-Hicks," SmartLiving365, accessed November 12, 2021, https://www.smartliving365.com/my-top-10-favorite-quotes-from-abraham-hicks/.
18. Catherine Moore, "Positive Daily Affirmations: Is There Science behind It?" Positive Psychology, March 16, 2021, https://positivepsychology.com/daily-affirmations/.
19. Kori D. Miller, "14 Health Benefits of Practicing Gratitude According to Science," Positive Psychology, September 10, 2021, https://positivepsychology.com/benefits-of-gratitude.
20. Milena Batanova (Harvard School of Education, research and evaluation manager), in discussion with the author, November 17, 2017.
21. Maureen Healy, *The Emotionally Healthy Child: Helping Children Calm, Center, and Make Smarter Choices* (Novato, Calif.: New World Library, 2018).
22. Maureen Healy, "Forgiveness: Are You Really Teaching Your Kids How to Forgive?" *Psychology Today*, September 27, 2010, https://www.psychologytoday.com/us/blog/creative-development/201009/forgiveness.

23. Ibid.

24. Johan Lind, Stephano Ghirlanda, and Magnus Enquist, "Social Learning through Associative Processes: A Computational Theory," *Royal Society Open Science* 6, no. 3 (2019), http://dx.doi.org/10.1098/rsos.181777.

25. Albert Bandura, Dorothea Ross, and Sheila A. Ross, "Transmission of Aggression through Imitation of Aggressive Models," *Journal of Abnormal and Social Psychology* 63 (1961): 575–82.

26. "The Practice of Forgiveness," Jack Kornfield's personal website, accessed November 12, 2021, https://jackkornfield.com/forgiveness-meditation/.

27. Oxford Reference, s.v. "empathy, n.," https://www.oxfordreference.com/view/10.1093/oi/authority.20110803095750102.

28. Belinda Parmar, "The One Crucial Skill Our Education System Is Missing," World Economic Forum, April 24, 2017, https://www.weforum.org/agenda/2017/04/one-crucial-skill/.

29. Judy Ho, in communication with the author, October 2020.

30. Mayumi Prins, in communication with the author, January 2013.

31. "InBrief: Executive Function," Harvard Center on the Developing Child, 2012, https://developingchild.harvard.edu/resources/inbrief-executive-function/.

32. Michelle Icard, *Middle School Makeover: Improving the Way You and Your Child Experience the Middle School Years* (New York: Bibliomation, 2014).

33. Michelle Icard, in communication with the author, March 19, 2018.

34. "Interview: Jay Giedd," Frontline, PBS, https://www.pbs.org/wgbh/pages/frontline/shows/teenbrain/interviews/giedd.html.

35. Michelle Icard, in communication with the author, March 19, 2018.

36. Ibid.

37. "What Is Compassion?" Greater Good Magazine, https://greatergood.berkeley.edu/topic/compassion/definition.

38. Ibid.

39. "Introduction," Frontline, PBS, January 31, 2002, https://www.pbs.org/wgbh/pages/frontline/shows/teenbrain/etc/synopsis.html.

40. "Executive Functioning Strategies to Tackle Homework," Dr. Ani & Associates, https://www.doctorani.com/single-post/2017/03/20/executive-functioning-strategies-to-tackle-homework.

41. Waguih William IsHak, in "The Science of Kindness," Cedars-Sinai, February 13, 2019, https://www.cedars-sinai.org/blog/science-of-kindness.html.

42. "Kindness Health Facts," Dartmouth College, accessed November 13, 2021, https://www.dartmouth.edu/wellness/emotional/rakhealthfacts.pdf.

43. Nancy Werteen, "The Kindness Curriculum: Can Kindness Be Taught?" 69News, February 25, 2020, https://www.wfmz.com/features/life-lessons/the-kindness-curriculum-can-kindness-be-taught/article_a5a74a66-5336-11ea-9a83-3b7736a2b4c3.html.

44. Ibid.

45. "The Children We Mean to Raise: The Real Messages Adults Are Sending about Values," Making Caring Common Project, July 2014, https://mcc.gse.harvard.edu/reports/children-mean-raise.

46. Debbie Goldberg, in communication with the author, November 2011.

47. Christopher Bergland, "The Neuroscience of Empathy," *Psychology Today*, October 10, 2013, https://www.psychologytoday.com/us/blog/the-athletes-way/201310/the-neuroscience-empathy.

48. Ronald Rohner, "They Love Me, They Love Me Not—And Why It Matters," YouTube, uploaded by TEDx Talks on June 15, 2017, 13:53, https://www.youtube.com/watch?v=6ePXxeGrfvQ.

49. Ibid.

50. Ibid., presentation slides.

51. Gayathri Chelvakumar and Scott Leibowitz, "Opinion: Bills Increase Stigma and Isolation Many Transgender Youth Feel, Doctors Say," *The Columbus Dispatch*, June 23, 2021, https://www.dispatch.com/story/opinion/columns/guest/2021/06/23/gayathri-chelvakumar-and-scott-leibowitz-bills-increase-stigma-isolation-many-transgender-youth-fee/5297432001/.

52. Child Mind Institute, "Transgender Children: A Mother's Story," Child Mind Institute, https://childmind.org/story/transgender-teens-mothers-story/.

53. Joseph G. Kosciw et al., *The 2019 National School Climate Survey: The Experiences of Lesbian, Gay, Bisexual, Transgender, and Queer Youth in Our Nation's Schools* (New York: GLSEN, 2020), https://www.glsen.org/research/2019-national-school-climate-survey.

54. GLSEN, https://www.glsen.org/.

55. Michael E. Newcomb et al., "The Influence of Families on LGBTQ Youth Health: A Call to Action for Innovation in Research and Intervention Development," *LGBT Health* 6, no. 4 (2019): 139–45, https://www.ncbi.nlm.nih.gov/pmc/articles/PMC6551980/.

56. Michelle M. Johns et al., "Transgender Identity and Experiences of Violence Victimization, Substance Abuse, Suicide Risk, and Sexual Risk Behaviors among High School Students: 19 States and Large Urban School Districts 2017," *MMWR: Morbidity and Mortality Weekly Report* 68, no. 3 (January 2019): 67–71, http://dx.doi.org/10.15585/mmwr.mm6803a3.

57. Child Mind Institute, "Transgender Children: A Mother's Story."

58. Suzanne Morris, quoted in Ronald Rohner, in communication with the author, September 10, 2021.

59. Ronald Rohner, in communication with the author, September 10, 2021.

60. Georgianna Kelman, in communication with the author, October 4, 2021.

61. Sabine Beecher, *Happiness: It's Up to You! Easy Steps to Self-Acceptance and Good Relationships* (Australia: Boolarong Press, 1998), 20.

62. Michael E. Bernard et al., "Self-Acceptance in the Education and Counseling of Young People," in *The Strength of Self-Acceptance* (New York: Springer, 2013), https://doi.org/10.1007/978-1-4614-6806-6_10.

63. Maria Montessori, in "Montessori Education," Montessori School of Oceanside, https://www.montessorischoolofoceanside.com/our-school/montessori-education/.

64. Donna Tetreault, "My Son Course Corrected—and Rediscovered His Love of Golf," *Your Teen Magazine*, accessed November 30, 2021, https://yourteenmag.com/sports/love-of-golf.

65. Pattie Fitzgerald's services can be found at her website: https://safelyeverafter.com/.

66. Rebecca T. Leeb et al., "Mental Health–Related Emergency Department Visits among Children Aged <18 Years During the COVID-19 Pandemic: United States, January 1–October 17, 2020," *MMWR: Morbidity and Mortality Weekly Report* 69, no. 45 (November 13, 2020): 1675–80, http://dx.doi.org/10.15585/mmwr.mm6945a3.

67. "Suicide Prevention: Facts about Suicide," Centers for Disease Control and Prevention, accessed November 30, 2021, https://www.cdc.gov/suicide/facts/index.html.

68. The Nielsen Company, *Battle of the Bulge & Nutrition Labels: Healthy Eating Trends around the World* (New York: The Nielsen Company, 2012), 3, http://silvergroup.asia/wp-content/uploads/2012/02/Nielsen-Global-Food-Labeling-Report-Jan2012.pdf.

69. Adekunle Sanyaolu et al., "Childhood and Adolescent Obesity in the United States: A Public Health Concern," *Global Pediatric Health* 6 (2019), https://doi.org/10.1177/2333794X19891305.

70. "Overweight & Obesity: Childhood Obesity Causes & Consequences," Centers for Disease Control and Prevention, accessed November 30, 2021, https://www.cdc.gov/obesity/childhood/causes.html.

71. Jeffrey Wakefield, "Obesity Could Affect Brain Development in Children," *Science Daily*, December 18, 2019, www.sciencedaily.com/releases/2019/12/191218153444.htm.

72. "Eating Disorder Facts," Johns Hopkins All Children's Hospital, December 21, 2020, https://www.hopkinsallchildrens.org/Services/Pediatric-and-Adolescent-Medicine/Adolescent-and-Young-Adult-Specialty-Clinic/Eating-Disorders/Eating-Disorder-Facts.

73. Sarah Stromberg, "Eating Disorders in Children and Adolescents," *On Call for All Kids*, Johns Hopkins All Children's Hospital, https://www.hopkinsallchildrens.org/ACH-News/General-News/Eating-Disorders-in-Children-and-Adolescents.

74. Katie Kindelan, "High School Senior Loses 115 Pounds by Walking to School, Changing Diet," *GMA: Wellness*, May 16, 2019, https://www.goodmorningamerica.com/wellness/story/high-school-senior-loses-115-pounds-walking-school-63047775.

75. American Psychological Association, s.v. "emotional security," https://dictionary.apa.org/emotional-security.

76. Peter Pressman, "The Science of Emotions: How the Brain Shapes How You Feel," *Verywell Health*, updated December 2, 2019, https://www.verywellhealth.com/the-science-of-emotions-2488708.

77. Rick Weissbourd, in communication with the author, March 9, 2020.

78. Judy Y. Chu, *When Boys Become Boys: Development, Relationships, and Masculinity* (New York: New York University Press, 2014), back cover blurb.

79. Vicki Zakrzewski, "Debunking the Myths about Boys and Emotions," *Greater Good Magazine*, December 1, 2014, https://greatergood.berkeley.edu/article/item/debunking_myths_boys_emotions.

80. Ibid

81. National Scientific Council on the Developing Child, *Young Children Develop in an Environment of Relationships*, Working Paper No. 1, p. 1, https://developingchild.harvard.edu/wp-content/uploads/2004/04/Young-Children-Develop-in-an-Environment-of-Relationships.pdf.

82. Ibid

83. K. Lee Raby et al., "The Enduring Predictive Significance of Early Maternal Sensitivity: Social and Academic Competence through Age 32 Years," *Child Development* 86, no. 3 (May 2015): 695–708, https://doi.org/10.1111/cdev.12325.

84. Angela Theisen, "Is Having a Sense of Belonging Important?" Mayo Clinic, December 8, 2019, https://www.mayoclinichealthsystem.org/hometown-health/speaking-of-health/is-having-a-sense-of-belonging-important.

85. Jay Davidson, "The Family Mission Statement," Child Development Institute, https://childdevelopmentinfo.com/family-living/family_mission_statement/#gs.b98usq.

86. "Forming Family Values in a Digital Age," Barna: Culture & Media, June 27, 2017, https://www.barna.com/research/forming-family-values-digital-age/.

87. "Forming Family Values in a Digital Age."

88. Sarah Conway, "How and Why to Write a Family Mission Statement," Mindful Little Minds, January 10, 2021, https://www.mindfullittleminds.com/family-mission-statement/.

89. Robin Berman, *Permission to Parent: How to Raise Your Child with Love and Limits* (New York: Harper Wave, 2014), 181.

90. Anonymous teacher, in communication with the author, April 20, 2018.

91. Dean Leav, in communication with the author, May 15, 2018.

92. World Health Organization, "Inclusion of 'Gaming Disorder' in ICD-11," September 14, 2018, https://www.who.int/news/item/14-09-2018-inclusion-of-gaming-disorder-in-icd-11.

93. Alan Mozes, "1 in 20 College Students Has 'Internet Gaming Disorder,' Study Finds," *U.S. News*, July 7. 2021, https://www.usnews.com/news/health-news/articles/2021-07-07/1-in-20-college-students-has-internet-gaming-disorder-study-finds.

94. Ibid

95. Anonymous mother, in communication with the author, May 9, 2018.

96. Anonymous mother, in communication with the author, May 10, 2018.

97. Gail Miller, in communication with the author, May 9, 2018.

98. Dani Roisman, in communication with the author, May 9, 2018.

99. Common Sense Media, https://www.commonsensemedia.org/.

100. Sierra Filucci, in communication with the author, May 16, 2018.

101. Gail Dines, in "Porn Talk: It's the New Sex Talk," *Kids under Construction*, podcast, April 30, 2020, 37:09, https://podcasts.apple.com/us/podcast/porn-talk-its-the-new-sex-talk/id1503083782?i=1000473116964.

102. "Internet Pornography by the Numbers: A Significant Threat to Society," Webroot, https://www.webroot.com/us/en/resources/tips-articles/internet-pornography-by-the-numbers.

103. Phil McGraw, in "Our Exclusive with Dr. Phil," NBC, February 14, 2019, https://www.nbcbayarea.com/news/local/our-exclusive-with-dr_-phil_los-angeles/8089/.

104. Donna Tetreault, "Giving Your Child the Power to Say No," LA Parent, January 8, 2018, https://www.laparent.com/parenting/the-power-of-no/.

105. Laurie A. Nimmo-Ramirez, in Ibid.

106. John O. Sullivan, "Why Kids Quit Sports," Changing the Game Project, May 5, 2015, https://changingthegameproject.com/why-kids-quit-sports/ Julianna W. Miner, "Why 70 Percent of Kids Quit Sports by Age 13," *The Washington Post*, June 1, 2016, https://www.washingtonpost.com/news/parenting/wp/2016/06/01/why-70-percent-of-kids-quit-sports-by-age-13/.

107. Tony Mazzocchi, "Why Students Really Quit Their Musical Instrument (and How Parents Can Prevent It)," The Music Parents' Guide, February 17, 2015, http://www.musicparentsguide.com/2015/02/17/students-really-quit-musical-instrument-parents-can-prevent/.

108. "Probability of Competing Beyond High School," NCAA, accessed November 30, 2021, https://www.ncaa.org/about/resources/research/probability-competing-beyond-high-school.

109. "2016 Draft Tracker," MLB, https://www.mlb.com/draft/tracker/2016.

110. Making Caring Common Project, https://mcc.gse.harvard.edu/.

111. Challenge Success, https://challengesuccess.org/.

112. Marilyn Price-Mitchell, "The Path to Leadership Begins in Youth," *Psychology Today*, September 26, 2019, https://www.psychologytoday.com/us/blog/the-moment-youth/201909/the-path-leadership-begins-in-youth.

113. Alison L. Miller et al., "Targeting Self-Regulation to Promote Health Behaviors in Children," *Behavior Research and Therapy* 101 (February 2018): 71–81, https://doi.org/10.1016/j.brat.2017.09.008.

114. Better Kid Care, "Leadership and Children," Penn State Extension, accessed November 30, 2021, https://extension.psu.edu/programs/betterkidcare/early-care/tip-pages/all/leadership-and-children.

115. Ibid

116. Ibid

117. Deepak Chopra, "Self-Compassion: Tips for Loving Yourself Just as You Are," The Chopra Foundation, June 22, 2015, https://choprafoundation.org/consciousness/self-compassion-tips-for-loving-yourself-just-as-you-are/.

118. Ibid

119. Centers for Disease Control and Prevention, "Autism Spectrum Disorder (ASD): Data & Statistics," accessed November 30, 2021, https://www.cdc.gov/ncbddd/autism/data.html.

120. Brigham Young University, "News Release: Parents' Comparisons Make Siblings Different," EurekAlert!, June 16, 2015, https://www.eurekalert.org/news-releases/769274.

121. Ibid

122. "Learn the Signs, Act Early: CDC's Developmental Milestones," Centers for Disease Control and Prevention, accessed November 30, 2021, https://www.cdc.gov/ncbddd/actearly/milestones/index.html.

123. Alison Escalante, "Parents' Love Goes a Long Way," *Psychology Today*, February 26, 2019, https://www.psychologytoday.com/us/blog/shouldstorm/201902/parents-love-goes-long-way.

124. Ibid

125. Mary Elizabeth Dean, "Family Love: What It Is, What It Looks Like, and How to Make It Happen," Better Help, November 12, 2021, https://www.betterhelp.com/advice/love/family-love-what-it-is-what-it-looks-like-and-how-to-make-it-happen/.

126. Robert J. Waldinger and Marc S. Schulz, "The Long Reach of Nurturing Family Environments: Links with Midlife Emotion-Regulatory Styles and Late-Life Security in Intimate Relationships," *Psychological Science* 27, no. 11 (2016): 1443–50, https://doi.org/10.1177/0956797616661556, cited in "The Importance of Family Love for Emotional Well-Being," ReGain Affection, August 3, 2021, https://www.regain.us/advice/love/the-importance-of-family-love-for-emotional-well-being/.

127. Suzanne Morris, in communication with the author, July 2020.

128. George Santayana, *The Life of Reason* (1905; Cambridge: MIT Press, 2011), 335.

129. Suzanne Morris, "The Inner Self Healing Journey" (unpublished manuscript, November 29, 2021), Microsoft Word file.

130. Suzanne Morris, in communication with the author, July 2020.

131. Morris, "The Inner Self Healing Journey."

132. Donna Tetreault, "Kids as Thrivers with Dr. Michele Borba," *Kids under Construction*, ABC4, podcast, March 1, 2021, https://www.abc4.com/podcasts/kidsunderconstruction/kids-under-construction-the-surprising-reasons-why-some-kids-struggle-and-others-shine-with-dr-michele-borba/.

133. Emmy E. Werner and Ruth S. Smith, *Journeys from Childhood to Midlife: Risk, Resilience, and Recovery* (Ithaca, NY: Cornell University Press, 2001).

134. Jade Wu, "5 Ways to Develop Self-Love, and Why You Need To," *Psychology Today*, July 29, 2021, https://www.psychologytoday.com/us/blog/the-savvy-psychologist/202107/5-ways-develop-self-love-and-why-you-need.

135. Ibid

136. Mark Guay, "Finding Purpose through Being Inspired ('In Spirit')," *HuffPost*, November 2, 2015, https://www.huffpost.com/entry/finding-purpose-through-b_1_b_8449822.

137. Name withheld, in conversation with the author, 2019.

138. Joani Geltman, in conversation with the author, 2016.

139. Katrina Schwartz, "Relationships Are Important: How Do We Build Them Effectively with Kids?" KQED, January 16, 2020, https://www.kqed.org/mindshift/55144/relationships-are-important-how-do-we-build-them-effectively-with-kids.

140. "About Us," Search Institute, https://www.search-institute.org/about-us/.

141. "The Developmental Relationships Framework," Search Institute, https://www.search-institute.org/developmental-relationships/developmental-relationships-framework/.

142. Michael J. Fox, "Family is not an important thing. It's everything," BrainyQuote, https://www.brainyquote.com/quotes/michael_j_fox_189302.

143. Encyclopedia.com, s.v. "expectation," updated May 17, 2018, https://www.encyclopedia.com/science-and-technology/computers-and-electrical-engineering/computers-and-computing/expectation.

144. Courtney E. Ackerman, "Pollyanna Principle: The Psychology of Positivity Bias," updated November 25, 2021, https://positivepsychology.com/pollyanna-principle/.

145. Ibid.

146. Dr. Michele Borba (@micheleborba), "Keep reminding your kids AND yourself," Twitter, September 25, 2021, https://twitter.com/i/web/status/1441816713989820423.

147. "What Chores Are Right for My Child?" Pathways, https://pathways.org/chores-right-child.

148. Yesel Yoon, "The Role of Family Routines and Rituals in the Psychological Well Being of Emerging Adults" (master's thesis, University of Massachusetts–Amherst, 2012), 2, https://scholarworks.umass.edu/cgi/viewcontent.cgi?article=2035&context=theses.

149. Ibid.

150. The Counseling Team, "The Importance of Celebrating During a Pandemic," Canadian International School, https://www.canadianinternationalschool.com/the-importance-of-celebrating-during-a-pandemic/.

151. Polly Campbell, "Why You Should Celebrate Everything," *Psychology Today*, December 2, 2015, https://www.psychologytoday.com/us/blog/imperfect-spirituality/201512/why-you-should-celebrate-everything.

152. Ibid

153. Kate Roberts, "Dr. Kate's Parent Rap: FAST Parenting; The Value of Flexibility," *The Salem News*, April 25, 2014, https://www.salemnews.com/news/lifestyles/dr-kates-parent-rap-fast-parenting-the-value-of-flexibility/article_cf869466-66f0-5ee9-b715-6b3ccd426e02.html.

154. "Flexibility Is Our Strength," Great Kids, accessed November 30, 2021, https://www.greatkidsinc.org/flexibility-is-our-strength/.

155. Roberts, "Dr. Kate's Parent Rap."

156. Donna Tetreault, "Co-Parenting Conflict During Coronavirus," *Kids under Construction*, April 2, 2020, https://podcasts.apple.com/us/podcast/co-parenting-conflict-during-coronavirus/id1503083782?i=1000470275309.

157. Ariadne Brill, "Flexibility: Building Block #8 for Positive Parenting," Positive Parenting Connection, February 19, 2013, https://www.positiveparentingconnection.net/flexibility-building-block-8-for-positive-parenting.

158. Reach Out and Read, https://reachoutandread.org/.

159. Ready4K, https://ready4k.parentpowered.com/.

160. Joseph A. Durlak, "The Impact of Enhancing Students' Social and Emotional Learning: A Meta-Analysis of School-Based Universal Interventions," *Child Development* 82, no. 1 (January/February 2011): 405–32.

161. Ronald Williamson, "Importance of High Expectations," Education Partnerships, https://oregongearup.org/sites/oregongearup.org/files/research-briefs/highexpectations.pdf.

162. Maria Montessori, "The greatest sign of success for a teacher . . ." BrainyQuote, https://www.brainyquote.com/quotes/maria_montessori_125856.

163. Maria Montessori, "Joy, feeling one's own value, being appreciate and loved by others," BrainyQuote, https://www.brainyquote.com/quotes/maria_montessori_752858.

164. Maria Montessori, "Never help a child with a task at which he feels he can succeed," BrainyQuote, https://www.brainyquote.com/quotes/maria_montessori_166858.

165. Lyelle L. Palmer, *Developmental Brain Stimulation in School and Day Care Settings: SMART Overview* (Winona, MN: Office of Accelerated Learning, Winona State University, 2003).

166. "Did You Know . . .?" Chess-Poster, https://chess-poster.com/english/notes_and_facts/did_you_know.htm.

167. Facebook user, identity withheld.

168. Anthony McGrann, "Should Educators in the Lower Grades Consider Eliminating Homework?" Seconds blog, April 29, 2012, https://seattleseconds.wordpress.com/category/homework/. See also: Challenge Success, "Changing the Conversation about Homework from Quantity and Achievement to Quality and Engagement," 2012, https://challengesuccess.org/wp-content/uploads/2015/07/ChallengeSuccess-Homework-WhitePaper.pdf.

169. Malibu High School, "Homework Policy—Guidelines," Parent Resources, https://www.smmusd.org/Page/1246.

170. Great Neck Public Schools, "Stress and Our Kids," October 2020, https://www.greatneck.k12.ny.us/site/handlers/filedownload.ataid=80897&FileName=StressandOurKidsOct2020.pdf.

171. Carol S. Dweck, *Mindset: The New Psychology of Success* (2006; New York: Penguin Random House, 2016), 10.

Acknowledgments

This book would never have made it out of my Google Docs folder if not for Lisa Sugarman, author of *How to Raise Perfectly Imperfect Kids—And Be Ok with It.* Lisa had just launched her book with Familius when she so generously asked me whether I had a book to pitch to the Familius CEO, Christopher Robbins. I told her my book wasn't ready, but she pushed me to submit it. She is why *The C.A.S.T.L.E. Method* is now out in the world. Thank you, my beautiful friend, Lisa.

Next, I want to acknowledge all of the people who allowed me to interview them, sometimes more than once: doctors, psychologists, educators, researchers, teachers, coaches, spiritual leaders, grandparents, and parents. I am in awe of your devotion to children and families.

Thank you to the entire staff at Familius. And a special shout-out to Kate Farrell, Brooke Jorden, and Shaelyn Topolovec: all of your kindness and guidance is greatly appreciated. Christopher Robbins, thank you for believing in this book, in all of its forms.

I am so extraordinarily grateful to my very talented editor, Tina Hawley. She is a compassionate teacher and has taught me so much. She helped structure this book to guide the reader to better understanding, making this book stronger via her spot-on editing. And much thanks to Spencer Skeen for his thorough copyediting.

I am so grateful to my mentors and friends. Dr. Phil, thank you for writing this book's foreword. I knew when I asked you that you would support me even amidst your incredibly busy life. You have always supported me, provided your time to me, and just been so fun to be around from our first meeting on. I take not only your career advice but your parenting guidance. You are a blessing in my life. Brad Bessey, my beautiful and supportive friend, you have always championed my work. You saw my dream to help create happy and healthy children and families via TV reporting. As executive producer of *Entertainment Tonight* and *The Insider*, you gave me opportunities to build on my personal goals as a parenting journalist when I walked away from general assignment reporting. You were there even when I doubted myself. You shared my vision. We shared our families. I am forever grateful to you. Dr. Michele Borba, when I first interviewed you for my podcast, it was inevitable that we would become fast friends. I thank you for all you do to lovingly back my work.

Thank you to all the executive producers who gave me a platform to share my work. Carla Pennington, executive producer of the show *Dr. Phil*, you are a powerhouse. I am in awe of the millions of people you have helped and educated via your role. Astra Austin, co–executive producer of *Dr. Phil*, you have always been so kind considering my pitches and ideas. You are a joy. Patty Ciano, executive producer of *The Doctors*, sweet Patty, thank you for always supporting me and my work. Rena Popp, executive producer of *Raising America* and supervising producer of *The Today Show*, thank you for allowing me to pitch you and pitch you! Thank you to all the TV news directors who allowed me to work as a parenting journalist when it was an "outside the box" idea. Bill Mondora at Fox 11, Tim Howick at NBC and Todd Reed at ABC4 Utah—amazing men and fathers.

Rick Weissbourd, psychologist and lecturer at Harvard, faculty director of the Making Caring Common project, thank you for supporting my work with young children via *Dear Me* and its corresponding curriculum. I'm honored.

Thank you to my mother-in-law and father-in-law, Nenelle and Brad. You have been wonderful parents and grandparents. Brad, I want to thank you for your insight and expertise as a literary attorney. Your guidance through the years has been an extraordinary gift. Nenelle, you have always supported me and have been there as a second mother. I think you know how much you mean to me. Thank you both for proofreading this book when I asked. Your expert eyes are greatly appreciated. And thank you to my Berkeley family. I love you all.

My deep thanks to my brothers and sister for being a part of my journey, both in childhood and as a mother, journalist, and author. You know me and love me for who I am. We are bonded forever. I love you all so very much.

Thank you to my parents. I got the best of the best. I was so blessed to have you as my mom and dad. Everything that you taught me and instilled in me I take along with me in life and in my role as mother. You both know how much I love and adore you; still, I want the world to know that you provided me a beautiful foundation along with the gifts of love, acceptance, and God. I would not be where I am today without all of your devotion and compassion.

And my final thank you is to my Andrew, my Jackson, and my Asher. You are my everything. I adore you all. Andrew, you believed in me when I didn't believe in me. And when I finally believed I could write this book, you supported me every step of the way. I have truly loved learning alongside you on our parenting path, on our life journey. Thanks for always being willing to try new things and work out issues together. Jackie boy, you are a gift from God. Your thoughtful, empathetic, and creative soul is bursting with love and kindness. My little, tiny Ash, God delivered you especially for me to show me how to live in my joy. My baby boys, you are my teachers. I love you, my beautiful family, and I love the castle we have created and continue to grow together.

About the Author

Donna Tetreault has been a national parenting/family/education reporter for over ten years. Before that, she was a general assignment reporter for CNN, KCBS-TV, and KNBC-TV, and an education reporter for KCBS-TV, relying on her expertise as a former teacher of kindergarten and first, fourth, and fifth grades. She has also taught journalism classes at UCLA Extension and been a guest blogger for Harvard University's Graduate School of Education's Making Caring Common Project.

As she moved into parenting reporting, she worked for NBC's CA Live, FOX 11 in Los Angeles, and HLN's Raising America with Kyra Phillips. She worked as a parenting contributor for *The Insider*, *Access Live*, and *Home & Family TV*. She writes for *U.S. News & World Report*, *Thrive Global*, *Your Teen Magazine*, and *LA Parent Magazine*. She has been seen on *Dr. Phil*, *The Doctors*, and *The Today Show*.

Donna is also the nonprofit founder of Caring Counts, whose mission is to teach kindness, compassion, self-compassion, and inclusion to kids and families, and which includes the "Kind Kid Warriors" initiative, promoting kindness via service-learning activities for children. For more information, check out www.CaringCounts.care.

Donna's debut children's book, *Dear Me, Letters to Myself for All of My Emotions*, is a Readers' Favorite Award Winner in the Educational Category and proactively teaches children positive mental-health strategies. She wrote and developed a corresponding curriculum which is now used in elementary schools across the country.

Donna lives in Los Angeles with her husband, Andrew, and their two sons, Jackson and Asher.

About Familius

Visit Our Website: www.familius.com

Familius is a global trade publishing company that publishes books and other content to help families be happy. We believe that the family is the fundamental unit of society and that happy families are the foundation of a happy life. We recognize that every family looks different, and we passionately believe in helping all families find greater joy. To that end, we publish books for children and adults that invite families to live the Familius Ten Habits of Happy Family Life: *love together, play together, learn together, work together, talk together, heal together, read together, eat together, give together,* and *laugh together.* Founded in 2012, Familius is located in Sanger, California.

Connect

Facebook: www.facebook.com/familiustalk
Twitter: @familiustalk, @paterfamilius1
Pinterest: www.pinterest.com/familius
Instagram: @familiustalk

The most important work you ever do will be within the walls of your own home.